"*Getting It Done* is a wealth of information for those interested in working in feature films and television. PA handbooks for commercials are a dime a dozen, but purchasing this comprehensive guide to the differing roles and responsibilities of PAs/ADs on long form productions will be a major score for up-and-coming PAs. The inclusion of standard production paperwork, directions on how to create an AD kit, glossary of terms, and the Paperwork Survival Guide alone are invaluable tools."
— Linda Burns, Producer, *The Little Death, Living Is Winning, The Signal*

"Joshua Friedman does a phenomenal job crafting his film experiences into the book that will become a production assistant's best friend, *Getting It Done.* To take it from Joshua: 'This book will offer you a foundation: It is up to you to adapt the knowledge for your own use.' Working in film, I can't imagine how to have written a better production guide."
— Amanda Porter, Associate Editor, *School Video News*

"The information the author presents is comprehensive and detailed, from job responsibilities of every production and crew member to all the equipment used. He includes extensive forms and checklists to get you familiar and organized, along with a glossary of terms from which to study. This PA's boot camp survival map prepares you to hit the ground running behind the scenes, before the action starts. It should be recommended reading for all film students."
— Ann Baldwin, Screenwriter, Blogger
(*http://ahigherfrequency.blogspot.com*)

"Friedman has laid out the basics of the entry level movie-set production world with clarity, humor, and a clear love of his subject matter. Production assistants armed with this manual should be able to start in the business just a shade less 'green.'"
— Sam Hoffman, Producer, Director, Author and Creator of *Old Jews Telling Jokes*

"The most complete explanation of the PA's work I have ever seen on paper. This should be required reading for anyone preparing to enter the world of on-set film production."
— Ann Ruark, Line Producer on *Revolutionary Road* and *Requiem for a Dream*

"Josh has created the ultimate PA bible. This is a must-have for anyone, PA or otherwise, who wants to excel in production and on-set. Relevant to big studio productions as well as indies. Great as an informative read or as a carry-with-you reference guide."
— Kevin Misher, President, Misher Films, Producer of *Public Enemies*

"For starting PAs, this is truly an invaluable resource. Friedman's writing smoothly details the inner workings of the job — and with true accounts that keep *Getting It Done* from being a dry read. At under 200 pages long, it can be read in a couple of days, and is thin enough to carry along and be referred to while on the job."
— Erin Corrado, *www.onemoviefiveviews.com*

"I recommend this book for *anyone* and *everyone* who works or interacts with a production office. Assisting an executive covering movies in production? Read this book. Representing writers working on a new TV show? Read this book. Still finishing school, hoping to soon make it to Hollywood as a director, designer, director of photography, writer, sound mixer, gaffer, or agent? Read this book. This is a fantastic guide to the nuts and bolts of every nook and cranny of a production office. If you want to understand how film and TV are made: *Read this book.*
— Chad Gervich, Writer/Producer: *Wipeout, Speeders, Foody Call, Reality Binge*. Author: *Small Screen, Big Picture: A Writer's Guide to the TV Business*

"If I'd had this book 15 years ago, I'd be running a studio by now. It will take over film schools."
— Kwesi Collisson, Producer, *Memoirs of a Teenage Amnesiac, Seven Days in Utopia*

GETTING IT DONE JOSHUA A. FRIEDMAN

THE ULTIMATE PRODUCTION ASSISTANT GUIDE

MICHAEL WIESE PRODUCTIONS

Published by Michael Wiese Productions
12400 Ventura Blvd. #1111
Studio City, CA 91604
(818) 379-8799, (818) 986-3408 (FAX)
mw@mwp.com
www.mwp.com

Cover design by Johnny Ink. www.johnnyink.com
Interior design by William Morosi
Edited by David Wright
Printed by McNaughton & Gunn

Manufactured in the United States of America
Copyright 2011 by Joshua A. Friedman

Library of Congress Cataloging-in-Publication Data

Friedman, Joshua A., 1984-
 Getting it done : the ultimate production assistant guide / Joshua A. Friedman.
    p. cm.
 ISBN 978-1-932907-88-9
 1. Motion pictures--Production and direction--Vocational guidance--United States. 2. Televi-
sion--Production and direction--Vocational guidance--United States. I. Title.
 PN1995.9.P75F75 2011
 791.430'232023--dc22
                                             2010031093

DEDICATION

I wrote this book for two of the most incredible people in my life, my grandfathers, Irving and Robert. Though they've passed on from this life, they've also passed on their love of learning and their desire to better themselves through education and experience. Thank you both, this is for you.

Of course, where would any of us be without an audience? This book is also dedicated to you, the PAs-to-be, who will carry on the torch long after I'm an Assistant Director pointing out to you what was pointed out to me.

TABLE OF CONTENTS

APPENDICES

ABOUT THE AUTHOR

ACKNOWLEDGEMENTS

This book has been an incredible experience for me. I have talked to so many interesting and knowledgeable people who have helped me gather information along the way.

First I'd like to thank my family. Mom, Dad, and Jenn, Grandmas Joan and Fran, and Aunt Carol, you folks have helped support and encourage me through this experience and have been an enormous comfort and resource.

Special thanks to my friend Adam, you have been incredible and thank you for putting up with my PA experiences!

Thank you to my mentor, John Roman, for giving me my start and teaching me the basics. Without the opportunity you gave me, this book would never have been possible.

Kathryn, if you had never told me "anything goes," I never would have made it this far. It's all your fault. Cheers!

Thank you Lisamarie, Jonathan, Paul, and Mark for your support, advice, and revisions. To Sydney for the use of her Paperwork Survival Guide. All of your help was invaluable in the creation of this book.

I can't forget Zach and his Zombies for providing me with my foundation of PA knowledge and for taking me off my lonely, crafty lockup. Thanks for the chance. Thank you to JJ for guiding me through the jungle we call Extras holding.

I offer my utmost appreciation to the entire crew of *Law & Order: Criminal Intent,* seasons 7 and 8. You guys are my home: Thank you for teaching me the wonders of this industry and how to do things right.

To Mare, Kara, and Brad, for teaching me to hone my skills and keeping me in line as I transitioned from television to film. The advice and experience I've gained from you has been invaluable

And mega-thanks to you, the PAs and ADs whom I've worked with over the years for showing me what to do and what not to do. Basically this book is a culmination of your teachings.

I simply say... Thank you.

FOREWORD

Twenty-two years old, I moved to New York City to find my way in the entertainment industry. Bright-eyed and bushy tailed, I stepped into the experience with one contact and no clue what I'd do or where I'd end up. I called my contact when I first arrived and told him I was looking for a job. He gave me the traditional "Welcome to New York" speech and that was pretty much where that ended. I was an actor in college. Maybe that could be a career. I went on auditions. Starred in a few short films. But it never went anywhere. I was living in New York City, acting for free, and bartending on the Upper West Side. What a way to start the career, right?

Every so often I would get discouraged along the path. At those times I would go to my parents' house in Atlanta to recharge away from the business and get my head on straight. One week under my father's guiding advice left me clearheaded with a goal in mind.

Back in New York, I applied for a job at a theater production house. It was a lighting rental house that also dabbled in production management. I balanced that job for $250 per week with the bartending job at night to pay my bills. I worked both jobs six days a week. My day off and my night off never coincided. To get to the place I wanted to be required a little sleep and a lot of work.

After six months of this crazy schedule, I had been a member of the production management team on 16 Broadway and Off-Broadway shows. I'd been sleeping roughly two to four hours a night and just could not function anymore. I decided it was time.

I've learned that in order to get anywhere in this business of entertainment you have to be able to take a risk. Just take the leap and pray that your feet hit something solid. This was my moment. I walked into the bar, quit on the spot, and focused on the theater work. I moved lighting equipment, built sets, cleaned, scraped, and painted many of the theaters in downtown Manhattan. In between

I'd listen in on phone conferences and watch business deals go down. I saw how much work went into theater and how little my employer was getting out of it and I had to reevaluate. I'd always been interested in film.

So I called up my family friend again and told him I'd been working in theater and bartending. I told him I was still looking to break into film if he had any suggestions. He said he'd see what he could do. I started looking for work anywhere I could.

Craigslist and Mandy.com had job postings and I found a few independent films and music videos I could work on. I signed on to a few and actually had more experience with my theater background than the crew did with their filmmaking. On most of these shoots I ended up working multiple jobs; a great experience, but still not what I wanted to be doing.

After two months of working for free and making little headway, I received a call from the Second (or, more commonly in the film industry, 2nd) Assistant Director on the TV show *Law & Order: Criminal Intent*. He offered me a low-level position as a "Production Assistant." I accepted, of course, and left the world of theater for a career in film.

Making movies has been an incredible experience for me. I've worked my way from the lowliest of the low to the big man on-set in some situations. All through observation and perseverance. Being a good PA requires a lot of patience and the ability to adapt and communicate quickly and efficiently. I've learned to balance, multitask, and work hard to rise quickly in this fascinating industry.

Now, two years down the road, I sit here and think: "Man, if I'd known then what I know now, I could've been a contender." Well, hopefully, with this guide you will be a top contender. So I wrote this book about my experiences that will help you become one of the best PAs in "the business." Good luck!

HOW TO READ THIS BOOK

This book started out as a group of discussions between myself and some green PAs in the industry. Green PAs are what we call new kids in the industry (they do not know what they are doing yet). These discussions turned into lectures, which one PA suggested I write down. And so I did.

This book is made up of all of the step-by-step explanations that I would share with the next generation of production assistants. If read from cover to cover, it will provide you with all of the skills that you will need to be successful and rise quickly. If you are a PA who has some work experience already, this book can be used to refresh or explain different aspects of the job. In this case it can be used as a reference guide.

The first section of this book will teach you about the different jobs on a film set. The second section will cover working on-set. The third section goes over the paperwork that you will encounter while working. The fourth section of this book offer tips and basics that PAs should know, and the final section offers advice on how to get a job.

Whatever your purpose for reading this book, I hope you find it useful and informative.

A NOTE ABOUT THE INDUSTRY

I personally see this business as a living, breathing creature. It is constantly evolving and growing. Because of this, I suggest that you remain curious, flexible, and innovative, always searching for new solutions to new problems. Ask questions of the people whom you work with. This book will offer you a foundation: It is up to you to adapt the knowledge for your own use.

THE GENDER ISSUE

Men and women have been working side by side in the film industry since the old days of the studio system. Things have improved drastically since those times (thankfully). In this book I have chosen to interchange the use of all masculine and feminine pronouns. Some PAs are male, some are female. This book is written for everyone.

A NOTE ABOUT LANGUAGE

This book was written to familiarize the reader with the language and terminology of the world of film. If a director asks for the location of an actor who is on the set, we will say he is "on set," not "on *the* set" as proper English dictates we say. The same will hold true when referring to different departments working on set. We do not call for "*the* Hair Department," we simply call for "Hair." Speech is kept short and sweet on-set; you'll be talking like a pro in no time.

In the world of film everything is abbreviated. This applies to the spoken word and the written word alike. Why say with a paragraph what you can accomplish with one sentence? The main titles that you will hear on set are "first AD," "second AD," and "second second AD." On a film set we will not write out the full titles as I have just done. Instead we replace the written word with its numerical equivalent. On the call sheet a first AD's title is listed as "1st AD," a second AD's title as "2nd AD," and a second second AD's title as "2nd 2nd AD." I have used the more commonly used forms in this book so that you can acquaint yourself with what you will see on a real working set. I know that you are eager to get on-set, so remember: Prepare today so you'll be ready to hear and read tomorrow.

It's PA 101

I once worked for an Assistant Director who had a very straight-to-business approach to work. Whenever an error was made, he would be there to right the wrong and explain to the Production Assistant (PA) what he or she had done.

On one of these days I happened to be standing near the PA who had made the error. She was a 1st Team (principal actors) PA in charge of labeling rooms and setting the sides (small copies of the script pages to be shot that day; they measure 8-1/2" x 5-1/2", and are folded to fit in a side pocket) for the actors when they came in. Apparently the rooms had been mislabeled and the actors never received their sides. Her excuse: "I was getting breakfast orders."

A Brief Note — Assistant Directors do not like to hear excuses. Just say "okay" and fix the error.

My AD friend explained to this PA the error of her ways and in one swift sentence drove the point home. He said "I understand you had other things to do, but this... is PA 101."

THE PEOPLE

THE PRODUCTION DEPARTMENT

I f you are reading this guide, you are obviously interested in becoming a Production Assistant (PA) in the fast-paced world of film and television. WARNING! This job is a commitment not to be taken lightly. It is intense, hard, and sometimes emotionally draining. This should not deter you from enjoying the thrill of filmmaking and the amazing experiences that you will have along the way. Just be aware, it's rough and tough. That being said, this section will give you an in-depth understanding of what will be asked of you in this business.

HIERARCHY OF A PRODUCTION DEPARTMENT

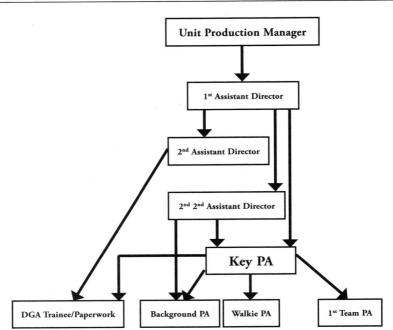

Everyone who's seen a movie knows the big names: director, producer, actor. But what do these people do? How do they affect the PAs? Truthfully, they have very little effect in the beginning.

The director deals primarily with the actors on-set. The producer works out of an office and comes to set to visit and make sure everything is running on schedule and under budget. The actors are there to do their obvious job... act.

So whom do you report to as a PA when you are on-set? That would be the Unit Production Manager and Assistant Directors.

UNIT PRODUCTION MANAGER

The Unit Production Manager (UPM) is the link between the producers and the set. He supervises all aspects of production including budgets, contracts, negotiations, and schedules. The job of a UPM is filled with long hours and constant communication with everyone involved in the project.

When questions arise on-set about breaking on time and shooting late, they are directed to the UPM. He will also be responsible for approvals on budgets and schedules to keep production on track. He will sign paychecks and authorize payments for rentals and purchases. It's a big job.

The UPM leads a double life. Half of his time is spent in the office working with vendors and the studio. The other half is spent on-set monitoring the day-to-day operations. In the office, the UPM will be supported by the production office coordinator. On-set he is supported by the assistant directors.

ASSISTANT DIRECTORS

Assistant directors are in charge of running the set. They are involved in production before the cameras are rented and the crew has been completely assembled. ADs are both planners and executors of the shoot on-set. They organize the schedule and coordinate between all departments to bring the project together. ADs come in three sizes: 1st ADs, 2nd ADs, and 2nd 2nd ADs (outside of the United States, these folks are called 3rd ADs).

● *1st AD*

At the top of the food chain is the 1st AD. He is the director's right-hand man. The 1st AD is responsible for the day-to-day running of the set. He is calling the shots and making sure that everyone is doing their job on time and correctly. A producer once told me there are two questions a 1st AD is constantly asking: "Why aren't we shooting?" and "What's wrong with this picture?"

As a good PA it is your job to answer these questions and solve any problems that arise. We are not shooting because:

• We're waiting on actors.
• Background needs to be propped up.
• We're setting lights.
• We need to run a rehearsal.

And the list of questions and answers goes on. Eventually you run out of answers and shoot.

• *2nd AD*

The 1st AD's second-in-command is the 2nd AD. The 2nd AD is responsible for scheduling the actors' arrivals and pickups as well as the logistics on-set. Logistics include calling in special equipment, stunts, special effects (F/X), etc. The 2nd AD's main duty is to prep the call sheet (covered in detail later) for the next day. In layman's terms, while the 1st AD runs the set today, the 2nd AD prepares (preps) everything for tomorrow.

Along with prep, the 2nd AD is responsible for secret excursions called photo shoots. It's pretty much like a real day on-set, except the people don't move as much. I'll go into photo shoots in more detail later, but for now, these can be the film industry's little goodies you can look forward to. You have the chance to observe the 2nd ADs and producers so that you can develop your own eye for what is a good shot and for what a shot may need. That can be anything from a slight nudge of the camera, a change in lighting, a shift of furniture, or the repositioning of an actor.

• *2nd 2nd AD*

Last, but most certainly not least, you will find the 2nd 2nd AD. This is the person who stands next to the 1st AD on-set and does the legwork. Her main responsibilities are to call the background (background actors) to and from set, make sure they are ready, and place them in their proper positions for the scene. On top of that she is responsible for ensuring that all paperwork from the previous day is correct.

All three ADs work together to ensure a smooth-running production. They will be relying heavily on you, the PA, to help make things happen successfully.

My First Fire Watch

My first day on-set was at a beach on Coney Island. I was assigned to a fire watch on my lunch break. Basically, I watched over the equipment while the crew ate their food. While I was sitting on the pier guarding the Sound and Prop carts, a beachgoer runs up and grabs two prop buckets. I yelled after him and he started yelling back, "I only want to borrow them! I need water for my sandcastle." I yelled back, "It doesn't matter what you need the buckets for! They're not yours!" He disregarded my warning and attempted to escape with my props. I chased him down the beach, tackling him to the sand in order to retrieve the stolen property. With the prop buckets safely back in my possession, the thief fled the scene of the crime. If a fire watch had not been in place... who knows where those buckets may have ended up!

My First Lockup

Lockups involve you in preventing someone or something from interfering with the working set. The best advice I can offer a new PA on a lockup is to have presence. I remember one of my first lockups in downtown Manhattan. An extremely large PA came up behind me to watch as a stream of oblivious people (mothers with strollers distracted by cell phones, tourists who didn't speak English, businessmen absorbed in conversation) blew straight through my lockup. I would say "Excuse me... ma'am... sir... could you... please... excuse me...." But nobody would stop. Finally the PA comes over and steps in front of me. I watch as a group of eight people head straight for our corner. He looks them in the eye, smiles, and makes a motion with his hands while saying, "Hey folks, just go this way for me! Thanks!" And they did! They actually listened. Why? He had presence. He was sure, he was confident, and remember: Body language works too. The more lockups you handle, the more effective you will become. No matter what, keep smiling and being nice: You are encroaching on someone else's neighborhood. Respect that and you'll be great.

PRODUCTION ASSISTANTS

There is a relatively small circle of working production assistants. Breaking in is the hard part. The purpose of this guide is to bring you up-to-speed so that when you do get that first job, you'll be prepared for whatever is thrown your way.

Most people assume that PAs are Gofers: Go for water, go for food, go for dry cleaning.... And while that is partially true, it is only a small part of the job. PAs are an invaluable asset to the set. We are the glue that holds the production together through all obstacles. PAs are in charge of extras, paperwork, crowd control, and many more things that come up throughout the workday.

We do everything needed for a production. What most people don't realize is that within the PA category are sub-categories of PAs; specialized jobs that serve a specific purpose. The PA hierarchy is as follows: Key PA, 1st Team PA, Background PA, Walkie PA, DGA Trainee (on non-DGA productions that would be the Paperwork PA), and Additional PAs. Each PA is responsible for different aspects of the set and all should work together to ensure a smooth-running production.

● *THE KEY PA*

The Key PA is in charge of running the PAs on-set. He hires additional PAs on big workdays and is the 1st AD's link to the rest of the PA staff. He is responsible for getting things done. The real question is, what should he do?

HIRING ADDITIONAL PAs

When hiring, you want to make sure to balance out your staff. While a strong experienced staff is ideal, you also want to hire some less-experienced PAs. Somebody has to raise the next generation, right? You will use your inexperienced (green) PAs for lockups (to be covered later) and errands, while your experienced PAs are in charge of running their respective teams and departments. The bottom line when it comes to hiring is who will do the job correctly, efficiently, and with the best attitude.

CREW SAFETY AND COMFORT

One of the Key PA's most important responsibilities is the safety of the crew. This means that when shooting in the street, the Key makes sure that traffic cones are properly set and pedestrians are properly diverted to keep the crew safe and working on schedule.

Know the set. The Key should know where the bathrooms are in every location; know where the controls to the air conditioning are so you can turn it off at the AD/Sound Department's request. A good Key will know all of the exits in a given location as well as any pertinent information that may come into play while shooting.

COMMUNICATING AND CONTROLLING THE CREW

The Key PA helps to facilitate the running of the set by translating orders from the higher-ups. The ADs will tell the Key what needs to be done and it is up to the Key to communicate that to the rest of the crew. As a PA, you will spread the message to department heads. Once you have relayed the message, let the ADs know that all parties involved have been "made aware."

The crew will either hate you or love you. Why do I say this? Because it is your job as the Key PA to keep them calm and quiet while working. They'll be banging ladders and C-stands around, while you're in the middle of a rehearsal where an actress must cry and needs absolute silence. That is why I want you to be prepared to be the bad guy. Sometimes, it's just that time.

The way the crew feels about you is totally based on the way that you deal with them. I choose a friendly approach. When I ask the crew to be quiet or tone it down, I first tell them, "You know better." No one likes to be talked down to and most of these folks have been doing this job since before you and I were born. For that simple fact, give them the benefit of the doubt. If you concede that they know what they're doing, and acknowledge that they know it's wrong, then you put the responsibility on the crewmembers and they're usually more inclined to listen.

SETTING LOCKUPS

Part of keeping the crew under control is setting lockups. A Key PA will approach the camera monitor and look at the frame (what the camera sees). Once the frame lines (the borders of the camera frame) have been established, he can figure out where to set PAs to effectively keep people out of the shot, while remaining off-camera themselves. He will then strategically place PAs around the set to keep pedestrians out of the shot. The Key will use traffic cones to block off sidewalks and street lanes while shooting, or use other obstacles to help direct and corral pedestrians around the working set. When shooting on a live street, the Key will have to coordinate a traffic lockup. This is done using officers from local law enforcement (in Manhattan, we call them TCD, or Traffic Control Department). TCD reports to the Locations Department, so the Key needs to communicate with the Locations Manager to arrange for them.

LOAD-INS/LOAD-OUTS

The Key PA is responsible for coming up with a plan to load the crew into and out of locations. Discuss this with the Locations Department and the ADs before the shooting day begins. Once the plan has been approved, the PAs will spread the message to all of the departments. If this is done properly, when the crew starts to roll out their heavy equipment, everyone will know where to go and nobody will complain or get lost. The same thing will apply for the load-out.

ASSISTING GUESTS

When guests arrive they are usually brought to the video village (the area where the director and producers sit to see what is being shot on a monitor) to watch the action.

If there is a guest on-set, the responsibility of getting them situated usually falls on the Key PA. This means talking to the Prop Department and getting extra cast chairs set up as well as talking to the Sound Department to provide a set of cans (a headset attached to a receiver that allows one to hear what the actors say into the microphone) for the guest.

EQUIPMENT STAGING

Another aspect of the Key's job is to tell the crew where they can stage their equipment safely, without being in the shot. To do this, the Key must talk with the 1st AD who will tell him where all of the safe places around the set will be. Items that will need to be staged include the video village, all carts and equipment, as well as extras that are not being used, and crewmembers who just like to look in the lens.

ORGANIZING THE VANS

At the end of the night, the Key is responsible for organizing van rides for background actors, cast, and crew. He will also assign PAs to trucks to get out-times (the time at which a department is off the clock). This requires the Key to know which trucks will need to be covered (have an individual looking after them) and delegate the responsibility of collecting out-times to the PAs accordingly.

IN SHORT

The Key PA has an endless job with many responsibilities too numerous to go into in this book. You'll learn on the job and, remember, every job is different.... Adapt. The best advice I can give you is to know the process on-set (this will be explained later), remain calm, and pay attention to what's going on.

The Hair and Makeup Dance

I was working on a movie in upstate New York and we were shooting stunt shots all day. I had six stuntmen and stuntwomen to get through Hair, Makeup, and Wardrobe. Here's where coordination and proper handling comes into play. After consulting with the Hair and Makeup artists, I sent the two women to their trailer. (Women usually take the longest, so you always want to send them to get ready first. I'm not trying to be sexist, it's just a fact. There's more to do!) Always ask first. I then asked the Wardrobe Department who they would like to see first. They too said the women. I explained that I had sent them to get their hair done and that I could bring them the stuntmen. Once a deal was struck, I brought three stuntmen into the Wardrobe trailer and the remaining stuntman to the Hair and Makeup trailer. When I got to the trailer, the women were finished with Hair and going into Makeup. I put my remaining stuntman in Hair and went to check on the stuntmen in Wardrobe. Two of them were ready, so I brought them to Hair and Makeup (arriving as the women had a minute left). I put one stuntman in the remaining Hair chair, and when the women finished I sent them to Wardrobe and put both stuntmen (hair now ready) into the Makeup chairs. I got my last stuntman from Wardrobe and put him in the Hair chair. The stuntwomen were ready, I had two stuntmen ready, and my last two took about five minutes in Makeup. Because I was patient and worked everything out among all three of these departments, we smoothly finished everyone in 45 minutes.

● *THE 1st TEAM PA*

The 1st Team PA is responsible for the 1st Team. In the industry that means principal actors. Principal actors include stars, day players, stunt players, and stunt coordinators. The 1st Team PA gets the actors comfortably situated in their dressing rooms, and brings them to Hair, Makeup, and Wardrobe before taking them to set for rehearsals and shooting. They are the ones responsible for the needs of the principal actors as well as any paperwork and contracts that may need to be signed.

COMMUNICATING WITH 1st TEAMERS

Communication is key in this industry. The 1st Team PA must keep the ADs informed about the whereabouts of each actor as well as their progress in getting ready for set. If an actor steps away from set, the 1st Team PA should be aware so that when the actor is called back, he knows where to look and is not scrambling and wasting time. Time is money and we already waste enough.

PAPERWORK

The 1st Team PA handles the principal actors' paperwork. He makes sure that contracts are signed and IDs are properly copied. He keeps track of the actors through a form called an Exhibit G (otherwise known as the "G"). This tells you what actors came in and which characters they played. It tracks the times that they: arrive, go through Hair and Makeup, arrive on-set, are released on-set, and when they actually leave. Actors must sign the G before they leave in order to be dismissed from set. The G is not the only responsibility of a 1st Team PA. An example of the Exhibit G can be found at the end of this section.

PRINCIPAL CAST MEAL PENALTIES

Principal cast members are entitled to receive meal penalties if they do not get a break from work every 6 hours. In order to avoid cast meal penalties we have three options. The first thing production may do is give the actor a nondeductible breakfast (NDB). If we break the actor within 2 hours of his call, then the 6-hour penalties do not go into effect until 6 hours from the time of the NDB. Production just saved 2 hours worth of penalties. Breaking an actor for a 1-hour lunch right at the 6-hour mark will also prevent penalties, and usually saves production 15 minutes to get the cast ready. They never really take a full hour to eat. If after lunch an actor must work for more than 6 hours, production has the option of breaking the actor for a second meal. This is usually a 30-minute break, because there is work to be done and we cannot afford to pay the crew meal penalties just to save some on the principal actors.

Cast Penalties: Cast members are entitled to a 30-minute meal break for every 6 hours of work. If the cast works past the break time, they receive the following compensation: Penalty 1 (30 minutes) awards the cast member $25, penalty 2 awards $35, and all subsequent penalties (30 minutes) award $50.

SETTING UP FOR THE ACTORS

The 1st Team PA arrives on-set and immediately checks all of the dressing rooms/trailers to make sure that they are clean and ready for use. He/she places sides (small script pages with that day's scenes) inside the rooms and labels them using the characters' names, not the actors'. We do this for two reasons: 1) we use character names for the safety and security of the actors and 2) so that the Wardrobe Department can set the costumes for the actors inside the rooms ahead of time. Once the rooms are all labeled, the PA will wait for the actors to arrive.

THE MORNING RITUAL — GOING THROUGH THE WORKS

The 1st Team PA announces the arrival of all actors as it happens. He keeps his Assistant Directors in the know. Once the actors have landed, the PA will knock on doors asking to take breakfast orders. While these orders are being made, the actors head to Hair and Makeup to get ready for set. The process of going through Hair and Makeup is known as putting an actor "through the works." The 1st Team PA keeps track of time. What time did the actors go into the chair? How long did it take? What time did they arrive? What time were they asked to come to set? After the actors are through with Hair and Makeup they will come back to their rooms, get dressed, and relax until the director is ready for them on-set.

INVITING ACTORS TO SET

The ADs will give the PA a warning before the actors are needed on set (usually 5 or 10 minutes). It is then the PA's job to pass this message on to the actors. Once the cameras are up and everyone on-set is ready, the actors will be invited.

Many ADs do not like to use the word "invite" when calling actors to set. This implies that the actor has a choice, when in fact they've been hired for a job. One alternative: "I've requested ____'s presence."

The 1st Team PA makes sure that a van or car is standing by for the actors to take them to set. He sees to it that all responsible departments (Hair, Makeup, and Wardrobe) are coming to set with the actors or right after. Anytime an actor is on-set to shoot, the above-mentioned departments must have a representative on-set as well.

BEING ON-SET

Once the actors are on-set, you (the 1st PA) stand by for them in case they need anything. Be prepared with water and some kind of snack in case they are hungry. Mints and gum are always a good idea, too. Have at least one set of small sides and one set of big sides in case actors lose their copies. Be sure to keep an eye on the actors while you are on-set. They will step away for a phone call or run back to their trailers without telling anybody. If you keep constant tabs on the talent, you'll be able to answer the Assistant Directors when they ask for the actor's location. On that note, an AD should never have to ask for an actor's location. If an actor decides to step off-set or run to Crafty (food service), let the ADs know over the walkie (short for walkie-talkie). You cannot control the stars; you can keep your boss in the loop.

STAY WITH THE ACTORS

If you have a lot of actors to work with, you may split the responsibility with an assistant. The assistant may stay with the actors on-set, and you may hang back with the ones in base camp getting ready for whatever is next.

A PA is always present to catch actors (called receiving an actor) on their way to and from set. Actors tend to get lost quickly: It is our job to make sure they know where to go at all times.

SET DISMISSAL

Once the actors have been dismissed for the day, they will go back to their rooms, change, take off their makeup, etc., and come find you, the 1st Team PA. They will have to sign out on the Exhibit G. When they sign you can present them with a call sheet for the following day of work as well as their in-time or report time marked and circled on the call sheet in big red Sharpie. Once that is done, the actors are free to go.

A side note to running (being in charge of) 1st Team: Always be prepared. Think ahead, anticipate, and know what is needed, what will be asked for, and how you can get it done most efficiently. Multitasking will save your life when the shit hits the fan... and believe me it will.

IN SHORT

To sum up the 1st Team PA's job, he is in charge of getting the principal actors ready for set, transporting them, and facilitating the completion of all of their paperwork.

Setting the Kraut

I was once working on a movie with Harrison Ford where he played a reporter at a sauerkraut festival. After Mr. Ford finished working for the day, the main unit left to shoot another scene. I was left back with the B-camera, the 2nd ADs, and 250 extras. Our instructions were simple; shoot some footage of the festival. I asked the AD what the frame of the shot was and he responded, "I don't know yet, just set something." (I think he thought I was an AD).

So I had 250 extras to play with. And boy, did I play. I pulled a few kids into a field and sat them down in a semicircle next to some bales of hay. I grabbed a clown and asked, "Please entertain these kids." And he did. I put a little girl on a tractor and introduced her to the actor who would play her father for the next 2 hours. "Honey, this is your pretend daddy, he's gonna help you play on this tractor." She's an actor, she understood. Next I organized a kraut-eating contest, placing some vendors at service stations and positioning festival-goers to look natural..

As I finished setting the festival the AD meeting broke up. As the ADs headed in my direction the 2nd Key began to shout, "Alright, let's start setting...." He looks around. "Never mind... let's shoot!" Imagine my pride!

Production Co:

Screen Actors Guild
Actors Production Report

EXHIBIT G

EPISODE NAME: _____

CONTACT: _____

PROD #: _____

PHONE#: _____

DATE: _____

DAY: _____ of _____

Worked - W
Finished - F
Started - S
Not Photographed - N/P

Rehearsal - R
Test - T
Hold - H
Travel - TR

W H
S F
R T
TR

CAST	CHARACTER	Dismiss MU/Hair Wardrobe	Work Time			MEALS						TRAVEL TIME					Stunt Adjust	Mileage	MPV OR FCS	ACTOR'S SIGNATURE
			Report On Set	Dismiss On Set	Dismiss MU/Hair Wardrobe	N.D. Brkfst OUT IN	1st Meal OUT IN	2nd Meal OUT IN				LEAVE FOR LOC	ARRIVE ON LOC	LEAVE LOC	ARRIVE AT HOTEL				

Assistant Directors: _____

15

● *THE BACKGROUND PA*

The "other" actors on-set are called background actors or extras. These are the people who are in the background of the scene and make everything look real. They are the Background PA's responsibility.

The Background PA has one of the few PA jobs on-set that not only involves logistics, but a little creativity as well. She is responsible for the paperwork of the background, preparing them, and sometimes setting them within a scene.

THE MORNING CHECK-IN

When background actors (background for short) arrive on-set they report to holding. This is a large room with some form of seating, a working bathroom, and plenty of water. Holding is the home base for the Background PA. When background comes to set they are given a form called a voucher which ensures that they get paid for the work they've done. Casting assigns each background actor a check-in number and the PA is given a set of "skins," which list each background actor's name, assigned number, the part they will be playing (e.g., police officer, jogger, student, etc.), and the scenes that they will play in. There are five main types of background actors.

TYPES OF BACKGROUND

• **Stand-Ins (SI):** Stand in the place of the principal actors while the shot is being set up and lit.

• **Special Ability/Photo Double (SA/PD):** Any special ability that is being used in the scene such as playing a sport, riding a bike, or a special talent (pole dancing, for instance) can be considered SA. Photo doubles stand in for insert shots. For example, when you see MacGyver pick a lock on screen, the hands that are used in the close-up may not be his. Doubles may also be used to cheat the shape of an actor from an angle where they will not be readily identified.

• **SAG Actors:** Union talent who get all of the privileges and protection that the Screen Actors Guild provides.

- **AFTRA Actors:** Union talent belonging to the American Federation of Television and Radio Artists.
- **Non-SAG Actors:** Any actor who is non-union and therefore not entitled to the provisions of a SAG contract.

GOING THROUGH THE WORKS

Once the background actors have checked in with the PA in holding, they need to have their outfits approved by the Wardrobe Department and their looks approved by the Hair and Makeup departments.

Some actors will need to be dressed by Wardrobe. If this is the case, contact your Wardrobe Representative and find out how they would like to dress the background. Sometimes they will come to holding; sometimes the background will go to the truck. In any case, if Wardrobe gives the background any items, they will need to hold onto a background voucher as collateral. As a PA it is your job to make sure that the background brings their vouchers to the truck.

Some actors will have to sit in the Hair and Makeup chairs. In this case you will most likely need a helper or assistant to manage the multiple tasks at hand.

PROPPING UP

After the background is approved, they will need to go to the Prop Department to get their props (any items they will handle or carry in a scene). This is known as getting the background "propped up." Follow the same protocol as with Wardrobe. Contact your Prop Representative and ask whether they would like to prop the background on-set, or at the truck. Once you have an answer, inform all the background that they must bring either their SAG cards or an ID with them. Again, this will be used as collateral for the props that they are given.

GOING TO SET

At this point your background is dressed, approved, and propped up. Now we just have to wait to be called to set! This part gets tricky. Background actors are not to be left to their own devices. They, like most actors, tend to get lost easily and it takes time to get them from point A to point B. Be prepared. Give the background their warning so they are ready to go when you actually call for them. (Be sure to check the bathroom for the stragglers.)

NONDEDUCTIBLE BREAKFAST AND MEAL PENALTIES
One of the biggest parts of the Background PA's job involves keeping track of in-times and scheduling.

If a background actor must travel to a location outside of the designated "zone," that actor's in-time will reflect the travel time it takes to get to location. This means that the actors' in-time will be earlier than the crew call and these actors will have to be broken (given a break) before the crew. To avoid this and balance the actors' break times to match the crew's break times, you can give the actors an NDB (Nondeductible breakfast; also used as a verb). An NDB is a 15-minute break in which actors must be given food. Production may NDB the background anytime within 2 hours of their call. NDBs are typically used 15 minutes prior to the crew call so that all breaks in the future are together.

For example: If the crew call is 8:00 a.m. and your location is a half-hour away, the background at the van will be on the clock at 7:15 a.m. The actors arrive on-set and get checked in. They are then NDB'd from 7:45 a.m. until 8 a.m. so that they are now breaking on time with the crew.

The purpose of an NDB is to avoid meal penalties. Every 6 hours the background actors must get a meal break from work. This is either a 30-minute catered meal or a 1-hour walk-away lunch. If the background is not broken at the 6-hour mark, they will receive a meal penalty (additional money paid for working past break time). It may be a penalty for production, but for background actors it is a nice bonus for a hard day's work. Each penalty increases in cost as time goes on, so the producer wants as little of these as possible. Because background actors come to set at different times throughout the day, their break times may be staggered. Some will have different lunches, etc.

Background Penalties: The break times are the same as with the cast; the difference is the penalty rates.

(The current value of background meal penalties as of the printing of this book.)

Penalty 1: $7.50

Penalty 2: $10.00

Penalty 3+: $12.50

As the Background PA, it is your responsibility to keep track of all these breaks and times and to inform the 2nd 2nd AD 30 minutes prior to the background actors going into a penalty situation.

ADJUSTMENTS

Background actors are paid for the items they bring. The first items a PA will see are wardrobe changes and some props (including moving vehicles). Actors get additional money (called a night premium — 10% of the base rate) for working past 8 p.m. They receive a double night premium (20% of the base rate) for working between the hours of 1 a.m. and 6 a.m. If they work in a wet scene or a smoky scene they get additional money, as well as bumps for going through special effects, Hair, and Makeup.

One note about bumps: They are like getting a bonus. The amount is in addition to the base rate. An adjustment is an amount that is calculated into the base rate and changes the hourly pay.

THE BACKGROUND BREAKDOWN

All of the above information regarding penalties, adjustments, and scheduling will be used to fill out the background vouchers as the workday progresses. At the end of the night you will need to organize these vouchers and complete a background breakdown form (the following example uses an alternate term: extras breakdown).

The breakdown is simple. It lists the number of background actors in each group; their rate, in-time, out-time, any overtime incurred, any meal penalties, and adjustments. The groups are organized by putting like vouchers together and are placed onto the breakdown in order. After you have separated and organized all of the groups, you must indicate which groups broke for lunch at what time, as well as a running total of stand-ins, special ability/photo doubles, SAG actors, and non-SAG actors.

The Background PA has a busy position. There are a lot of rules and guidelines to follow, but it is great training for work as a 2nd 2nd AD.

INSTRUCTIONS FOR ORGANIZING THE BACKGROUND BREAKDOWN:

1. Group all vouchers that are exactly the same into piles.
2. Paperclip the piles so they stay organized.
3. Take one pile at a time and fill out one sticky note per pile.
4. The sticky notes should contain all of the following information:
   a) Number of Vouchers @ $$ (Pay rate)
   b) In-Time
   c) Out-Time
   d) Total Hours Worked
   e) Overtime Hours (anything over 8 hours for SAG or AFTRA)
   f) Lunch Times
   g) Meal Penalties Incurred
   h) Adjustments
5. Now you organize the piles with their fresh sticky notes in the following order:
   a) Highest Rate
   b) Most Hours Worked
   c) Most Adjustments (in dollars)
   d) Most Meal Penalties
6. Once all this is done, transfer the appropriate information from your sticky notes to your background breakdown form. And that's all!

Show Title
Extras Breakdown

Date:
Show Title
Day ___ of 8

Number	Rate	In	Out	OT	MVP	Adjust.	Misc.

Totals		SI@ Rate =____	Lunch 1 = __ = _____			
		Photo Dbl@ Rate =____	Lunch 2 = __ = _____			
		SAG@ Rate =____	Lunch 3 = __ = _____			
		NonSAG@ Rate =____	Lunch 4 = __ = _____			
		Total BG =____	Lunch 5 = __ = _____			

Day Rates		Adjustments	Meal Penalties	Wardrobe Rate	
Stand- In: $		Wet/Smoke: $14	1st Penalty: $7.50	Police Uniform : $36	
Photo Dbl: $		Luggage : $5.50	2nd Penalty: $10	Formal/ Uniform: $18	
Sag : $		Auto, 30c per/m: $35	Addtl. Penalty: $12.50	1st Change : $9	
Non Sag: $		Bicycle : $12		Addtl Change : $6.25	

Key: N=Night, W=Wet, A=Auto (specify tolls and mileage), C=Change, F=Formal, U=Uniform, P=Prop (specify)
        WLK=Walkaway, NDB=Nondeductible Breakfast

● *THE WALKIE PA*

The Walkie PA is the entry level job in the PA world. He is responsible for distributing walkie-talkies to all of the crew along with headsets and batteries. He also doubles as the Key's right-hand man. With no structured responsibilities to tie down the Walkie PA, he is free to help out wherever the Key needs it on-set.

THE WALKIE-TALKIE

The first thing you should know is how a walkie-talkie works. Push

the button and talk. This is how all PAs communicate. We use 16-channel shortwave radios or walkie-talkies. The current standard model is the Motorola CP200 and usually has 16 channels (which can be switched by turning a knob) and a volume knob. To talk, push and hold the button on the side. If your headset is plugged into the walkie, the button on the side of the walkie will not work: Use the button attached to your headset.

CP200 Walkie © *Mark Romanelli* 2009.

BATTERIES & EXTRA WALKIES

As a Walkie PA, be aware of what will be needed during the day. You are in charge of keeping hot batteries ("bricks" or "biscuits") on-set. Make sure that every PA has one hot (charged) brick at all times. If you have picture cars moving, you may need walkies in them. When stunts are on-set, a medic will need a walkie. Ask your Key how many additional PAs will need walkies. What special effects experts are coming in? How many walkies will they need? These are all things you should think about as a Walkie PA.

THE BRICK BOX

You have the option of either building a brick box for hot and cold (dead) batteries, or keeping two separate bags; one for hot bricks and one for cold. This ensures that batteries don't get lost or wasted. I've seen some boxes with wheels, and some with closable lids. Some of the boxes are simply walkie cases marked with tape that says "hot" or "cold." However you choose to store your batteries on-set, it will be your job to keep a running count of what you have available.

HEADSETS

The Walkie PA must know all about his equipment. There are three main types of headsets used.

The first is called a BK or McDonald's headset. It looks like the type of headset you see on a fast food drive-thru employee. Be careful with these headsets. You can accidentally press the talk button without realizing, and then everyone on Channel 1 will have just heard about the massive indigestion you had this morning. This pitfall of the BK headset is known as "cueing."

The second type you will see is a hand mike. Hand mikes are used more by the Locations, Grip, and Electric departments. They clip to your body and act as a low speaker/microphone.

The third and most coveted headset is the surveillance headset. It wraps around your ear and fits inside comfortably. It comes with either one wire or two. I prefer the two-wire model, as it allows for more mobility.

Headsets: © *Mark Romanelli 2009.*

ADDITIONAL RESPONSIBILITIES

While you are taking care of all the walkie needs, you will be called upon to help the Key PA lockup the set (lockups will be covered in more detail later). You will also be sent on runs for anything from coffee to batteries, and more often than not will be the first person to come in the morning to pick up paperwork (known as *distro,* for distribution). Paperwork includes the sides (small copies of the script pages to be shot that day) as well as contracts, memos, and dailies (DVDs with the previous day's scenes exposed for review). The Walkie PA will also gaff (load people into a van) the first van leaving to location in the morning.

IN SHORT

The key to being a Walkie PA is knowing your inventory and keeping track of who has what. Make sure that everything comes back to you and check and recheck as needed. If things break, send them back immediately. The rental company will repair or replace any and all defective equipment. Stay on your game and you'll be fine.

DGA TRAINEE/PAPERWORK PA

The DGA Trainee/Paperwork PA is vital to a production. He/she has a very big job to do and it involves knowing almost everyone working on the production. Before I explain what the trainee or Paperwork PA does, I'd like to tell you about the DGA and the DGA Trainee program.

DGA TRAINEE PROGRAM

DGA stands for Directors Guild of America. The guild consists of Unit Production Managers (UPMs), Assistant Directors (ADs), and directors. To join the guild and work as an AD or a UPM, a Production Assistant must have 600 workdays of experience as a PA on a union set. If you'd like to get into the guild faster than that, you can apply to the highly competitive DGA Trainee program. This program teaches you the skills you will need to manage a production. The competition is stiff, and the selection process takes months, but the knowledge and experience you will gain is invaluable. If you don't get into the program, do not worry! I took the test twice and didn't get in… so there's always another way.

THE PAPERWORK JOB

Paperwork PAs are the ADs of the PA world. They help to coordinate and record the events of both the shooting day and the preparations beforehand. These PAs have numerous responsibilities; they take manpower (list each crewmember working that day), record the times each scene starts and is completed, order lunch, and coordinate traffic between the office and the set. The job is stressful and the hours are the worst on-set, but I can't think of a better way to learn the business side and prepare for the next step; assistant directing or producing.

The advantage to being a Paperwork PA is found in the freedom away from set. The Paperwork PA is always busy gathering information from other crewmembers. He gets a chance to speak and listen to almost everyone on-set on a daily basis. Because of his numerous responsibilities, the Paperwork PA is rarely called to set for lockups (preventing passersby and non-film cars from entering a scene shot on location). This allows him to learn how the set runs and understand how shoots are planned.

YOU WORK FOR THE 2nd AD

Paperwork PAs work for the 2nd AD. Whatever they need, it is your responsibility to get. You will spend a lot of time in the production office with the 2nd AD. Learn how to read their moods. If it seems like there is a stressful situation brewing, ask if you can help once, and then leave the ADs to their work. If they need you, they'll ask.

COLLECTING MANPOWER

One of the main paperwork jobs is collecting the manpower (creating a daily list of all crewmembers working). To collect the manpower you will have to talk to each department individually. Here's a list of who you should talk to in each department:

- Hair — Key Hair Stylist
- Makeup — Key Makeup Artist
- Wardrobe — Wardrobe Supervisor
- Production — Key PA
- Camera — 2nd Assistant Cameraman
- Sound — Sound Utility or Mixer
- Grip — Best Boy Grip
- Electric — Best Boy Electric
- Props — Prop Master or Assistant Prop Master
- Scenic — Scenery Artist (usually a one-person department)
- Scripty — Script Supervisor (there's only one on-set)
- Set Dressing — Head Set Dresser
- Rigging Grips — Rigging Key
- Rigging Electrics — Rigging Key
- Transpo — Teamster Captain

As I've worked more and more I've realized that text messages are an awesome thing. A lot of times I may not be able to track crewmembers down to ask them for the manpower. If I send them a text, they'll respond quickly and I'll have a record of the exchange. G-d, I love technology.

THE PRELIM

After the manpower is complete, you will wait for the 2nd AD to give you a prelim (preliminary call sheet). Go over the prelim with a fine-tooth comb. If you find any mistakes or have any questions, bring them to the AD's attention immediately. Next the prelim is copied on yellow paper to differentiate it from an official call sheet. The copies will be handed out to key members of the crew so that they may begin working out a plan for the following day's shoot. The prelims should be given to producers, ADs, all department heads, and staff PAs.

COUNTING AND CALLING LUNCH

It's almost that time, so let's go check in on lunch. It's your responsibility to verify if or when lunch is ready. Once the crew breaks, you will stand at the front of the lunch line and count the number of people who go through to eat. At the end of lunch you will compare your number with the caterer's; hopefully they match. Sometimes you will have to kick people out of line if they are not with the crew. Producers don't like to pay for people who don't work for them, and catering charges per head.

There are two rules a PA must follow when breaking for lunch:

1: Crew must eat before background actors.

2: The back-in time from lunch cannot be called until the last crewmember has gone through the lunch line.

Once the last crewmember goes through the lunch line, find the shop steward (the local representative of the International Alliance of Theatrical Stage Employees — IATSE — for the production). Show him the time on your watch and he will give you a back-in time that is exactly 30 minutes from that point. If lunch is a little far from set, the shop steward will give you a back-in time that includes the time it takes to travel back to set. Since you know the back-in times, you should walk around to each table in the lunch-room and politely let them know that "the company will be back-in at 'X' time in catering and back-in at 'Y' time on set." Once the lunch is over and everyone has eaten, talk to the caterers and get the lunch receipt. Save the receipt for your file at the end of the day.

PREP THE PRODUCTION REPORT

After lunch, try to spend some time on-set. Help out the team and get to know the crewmembers that you don't normally spend time with. This time can also be used to prepare (prep) your production report for the end of the night. This means getting a head start on your production report by adding any pertinent information from the day's call sheet.

THE CALL SHEET

About an hour before wrap (finishing time), the 2nd AD will hand you a call sheet to copy. Scan the call sheet like you did the prelim for any potential errors. Pay special attention to the transportation section. If you find an error here, you may have just saved production from picking up an actor at the wrong time. Once you've proofed the call sheet, the AD will get it signed and you will make enough copies for the entire crew.

Once you copy the call sheet, distribute the copies as follows:
- The first copy goes to the 2nd AD.
- The next five to ten copies go to the Teamster Captain.
- Save five call sheets for yourself in the office.
- Save the 1st Team PA enough call sheets for the cast, and the Hair, Makeup, and Wardrobe departments.
- Bring the rest of the copies to the Key PA to distro at wrap.

After the call sheets are on-set, wait for the ADs to yell, "Wrap!" Now the fun begins!

COLLECTING OUT-TIMES

At wrap, it is the Paperwork PA's job to collect the out-times. The Key PA will assign a PA to watch over every department and collect an out-time from them when they are done working for the day. The PA will report that out-time to the Paperwork PA, who will type it into the production report. While the out-times are being collected, different crews will drop off different pieces of paperwork for the production report.

NIGHTLY PAPERWORK

The end of the night is like a puzzle for the Paperwork PA. All the pieces will come together. You already have the catering receipt!

The Camera Department will drop off the camera reports and the film inventory log. Each report contains information about the film stock that was used; how much film was loaded, how much was good, how much was wasted, and how much was re-canned (re-canned film is known as a "short end"). The inventory sheet summarizes all of the information on the camera reports and adds it to the running film counts. As technology progresses and the industry switches to more digital systems, camera reports adapt as well. When working on a digital shoot, camera reports will record the number of clips (takes) shot and the amount of footage (in gigabytes).

The Sound Department drops off sound reports. These reports are for the sound mixer. They look like a grid and list the track numbers of each take as well as whether the recording was on a boom mike or a body mike. The report will also list any wild tracks (sound with no accompanying image, used to turn background sounds into white noise) that were recorded that day.

The Script Supervisor will hand in the script notes. The notes summarize every shot and every take. They also contain all of the times that a Paperwork PA needs to report to the office. These include the first shot, the first shot after lunch, and wrap times. The script notes will keep a running total of everything that has been recorded to date, so that anyone looking can see how much of the project is left to be shot.

The 1st Team PA and the Background PA will turn in the Exhibit G and the background breakdown, respectively. Your contribution to the paperwork at the end of the night will be the original signed copies of the call sheet and a printed copy of the production report once it is complete.

In Appendix D you will find a Paperwork Survival Guide.

Make it Seamless

I was once working on a production in White Plains where the base camp was about a mile away from the set. The copy machine was kept in base camp and the AD whom I was working for set up his base on-set. I would travel back and forth between the two all day, running errands and the like. One day the AD gives me the call sheet 20 minutes before wrap. I take the papers, get in the car, drive to base camp, then realize I'd grabbed the wrong papers.

What do I do? If I go back to get the call sheet I look like an idiot, and it will take too much time to drive there and back, let alone print the thing. Then the light bulb went on.

If I can't bring the call sheet to the copier, I'll bring the copier to the call sheet! I picked up this hunking copy machine and put it in the trunk of the production car. I then drove to set and ran to the AD base, copier in hand. The AD looks up from his desk to see me with my trusty copy machine, running full speed. I manage to get out "Grabbed... wrong... sheets," as I plugged in the machine and started copying the call sheet. His only words: "Make it seamless."

The Infamous Film Drop

There exists a story that every PA in New York can tell you. It goes like this:

At the end of every day on-set, all of the film that has been shot is handed to a PA to be delivered to the film lab for processing. On one such Friday night, a nameless PA was told he'd be making the film drop. Soon after he was told that the PAs were going to a bar to drink and that he should come. Thinking it through, the PA decided the film could wait. The lab wouldn't process it until the morning and the lab is open all night. One or two drinks can't hurt. So our nameless PA goes out to the bar. He has a few drinks, he has a good time. He picks up the film, pays his tab and gets in a cab. The cab takes him all the way home where he pays for his ride and bids the driver goodnight. He waves as the film from that entire day's shoot disappears into the night air, never to be heard from again. It's a lesson that is used to scare all new PAs into being careful and responsible. And it's a true story.

● *ADDITIONAL PRODUCTION ASSISTANTS*

Additional Production Assistants are the worker bees of the PA community. These are the folks who are either starting out or working on multiple projects and have the flexibility to work as daily hires. While an additional PA will rarely be given specific responsibilities like the Staff PAs we have already discussed, they are vitally important to the running of the set and to your training as a Production Assistant. There are three main types of additional PAs.

LOCKUP PAs

The Lockup PA stands at a street corner and tells people that there is a project shooting in this area and it's not okay for them to walk through our shot. They will also look for the source of loud noises, such as the beeping of a truck backing up or a jackhammer at a construction site. Once the source of a noise is found, we try to get the source to work with the crew and keep the noise down while the cameras are rolling. After the Lockup PAs come the runners.

RUNNERS/DRIVING PAs

The runners are PAs who do just what the name says. They go on runs if an actor needs coffee, a director needs breakfast, or someone left something at the last set. The runner runs around all day making pickups and drop-offs. Along with the runners are the Driving PAs, who are responsible for driving on low-budget shoots.

HELPERS

The most coveted of the additional PA positions is the assistant or helper position. The 1st Team helper or the background helper is the Staff PA's right-hand assistant while working. He or she will be right next to the action with a great opportunity to learn and grow. Try to befriend a staff member who can recommend you to be one of their assistants. It's the best way to move yourself up fast.

Dead Bodies and Water Bottles

When you work on a procedural show like *Law & Order* or *E.R.*, you will notice events that happen in every episode of the series. There will always be a criminal and there will always be a victim. In my case I noticed that the victims we used were playing corpses for hours at a time without a break. These actors were made to look dead and sit on a cold slab for a few hours while we shot the scene. They could not eat or drink because that might result in smeared makeup. I saw this problem and devised an effective solution.

In true MacGyver fashion, I used a water bottle, a key, and a bendy straw to build a drinking device that would not leak on actors in a horizontal position. Here's the trick:

Take the water bottle and make sure that the plastic cap is screwed on tightly. Take your key and point it down into the center of the bottle cap. Press and twist the key all the way around and back continuously until it breaks through the cap. Hollow out the hole until it is slightly smaller than the diameter of the bendy straw. Slowly and carefully force the straw into the hole until it hits the bottom. Now when you gently pull up on the straw, the plastic of the cap should hug the outside of the straw, forming an airtight seal. Tilt the bottle sideways and test it. No drip, huh? Now the "corpses" could quench their thirst while waiting for the cameras to roll. Thus the problem was solved using the MacGyver leakproof water bottle.

WORKING CREWS

Being a PA is all about "The What." What to do. what to look for, what to observe. But you also need to know "The Who." Knowing what you need to do doesn't help if you don't know who to talk to in order to make things happen. In this section I'll go over a brief description of each of the crews on a film set, the players involved, and what each department is responsible for in relation to the job of a PA.

Let's start with the departments that have the most contact with PAs and we'll work back from there.

HAIR, MAKEUP, AND WARDROBE

Hair, Makeup and Wardrobe are three separate departments but they all cooperate in working towards the same goal: Get the actors ready to be in front of the camera. Hair will style, color and/or trim anything on top of the head. Makeup is responsible for the normal face touch-ups as well as more extreme makeup. What may you ask is extreme makeup? The illustration below of a scar is from the TV show *Fringe*. In the scene an elevator plummets to its doom with multiple passengers inside; this scar is the result of that accident. Cool, huh? This is a case of extreme makeup.

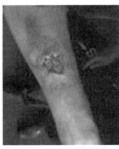

This body makeup was used on the show *Fringe* after an elevator plummeted to its doom with this woman inside. © *Joshua A. Friedman 2009.*

Scars, wounds, autopsy incisions: Makeup is responsible for all of these things. They are also responsible for facial hair. Makeup will trim, shave, and neaten any facial hair as needed.

The last leg of this tripod is the Wardrobe Department. They are responsible for all the clothes the actors wear. They check the wardrobe of the background. They set clothes in the actors' trailers; they keep extra outfits just in case an accident happens. These three departments are the actors' support system, the last system of checks and balances before the actors put their looks in front of the camera.

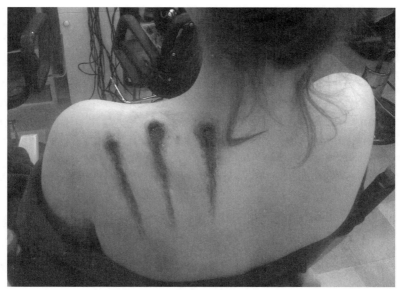

Pictured here is the victim of a small garden rake. The scratches look real! © *Joshua A. Friedman 2009.*

● THE PEOPLE

The heads of the Hair and Makeup departments are called the Keys (just like the Key PA). The Key Hairstylist and the Key Makeup Artist are the people whom the PA should look for. Any question you have in regards to these departments should be fielded to these persons. Knowing whom to speak to in the Wardrobe Department gets a little trickier.

The head of the Wardrobe Department is called the Wardrobe Supervisor. The supervisor organizes the day's wardrobe setups and assigns set costumers to get the actors dressed, checked, and prepared. Now here's the tricky part. The set costumers are each responsible for a different group of actors. One costumer is responsible for the main stars. A second costumer is responsible for the day players. And a third costumer checks all the wardrobe that the background will wear on camera.

● LAST LOOKS

Why does this information affect a PA? Last looks! What are last looks? They are the final stop on the road to shooting. After all the rehearsals, before the camera rolls, a representative from Hair, Makeup, and Wardrobe will give the actors a last inspection for any flaws or missing details before shooting starts.

● *KNOW THE TEAM*

Your job as a PA is to keep track of these elusive people. Get to know them, learn their names, and know what to ask of each of them. Some hairstylists and makeup artists may only be brought in to work on background. Some Wardrobe Supervisors are the only ones allowed to work with a certain actor. If you understand how responsibilities are divided among these three departments, you will be better prepared as a PA.

● *A RULE OF THUMB*

When understanding what each department is responsible for, here's a good rule of thumb:
• Hair takes care of the top of the head.
• Makeup takes care of the face and any body parts that show skin.
• Wardrobe deals with clothing the body… from the hats to the shoes.

So top to bottom; Hair, Makeup, Wardrobe.

LOCATIONS

The Locations Department (notice Locations is plural) can be your best friend on-set or your worst enemy… it's your call. Their job is to scout and find locations to shoot in, secure proper permission, and learn the layout of the set. They find bathrooms and restaurants, form relationships with building owners, managers, and custodians, and take care of general maintenance and care of the property.

● *LOCATIONS — THE PEACEKEEPERS*

Locations is basically production's window to the world. If there is an argument on or near the set, Locations are the people you call. If a neighbor has a complaint, Locations will find a solution. When the dance hall above the restaurant you are shooting in refuses to turn their music down, as was the case one night on *Law & Order*,

Locations steps in to mediate. They will also help track down any noise or sound that the Sound Department is hearing on their microphones and help get it turned off.

Besides dealing with the actual shooting site, Locations secures a holding area for the background as well as a catering hall for the crew. They put signs up to direct crewmembers to all locations and catering, mark bathrooms, and let the crew know about hazards or when it's not okay to bring food or drink to a set.

THE PEOPLE

Within this department there are many jobs. At the top of the list are the Locations Manager and the Locations Coordinator. These people go on scouts with the producers and directors to check locations and find something that pleases all involved. Next there are the Assistant Locations Managers. These folks do just that. They assist the Locations Manager and are the top dog on the physical set. There are two people who you may not see on-set. The Locations scouts visit locations ahead of time to secure them for future shooting. The Prep/Wrap PA comes into a location once it has been secured. He supervises the set dresser and rigging crews as they prep for the shooting crew that will follow. After production is finished with a location, the Prep/Wrap PA will oversee the load-out of the location. Under the Locations Manager are the Locations PAs. These are the grunts of the Locations Department and a PA's best friends. These folks put the signs up, take out the trash, get directions, and most importantly, they locate and stock every bathroom on-set. They even set up the tables and chairs for the crews to have lunch. Basically, they assist with anything you could want in regards to the location itself. Get to know them. They will help make you aware of what is going on with the location so you, the PA, will have an answer when a problem arises.

Making Mistakes

As a PA you will make mistakes: It's inevitable. You won't make them on purpose of course, but you will make them and you will learn from them. During my second week ever on a film set I was asked to walk to the next location and confirm that the SWAT van had landed and was ready for the next scene. Eager to prove myself, I hurried over and scouted the set. I did not see anything that resembled a SWAT van. Not to panic, I checked the street. No van. I looked around the corner and saw it. Across the street was a van with police lights on top, a cage door I could see through the window, and a shotgun rack. This was it! As I approached the van I realized it had been blocked in by six police cruisers.

Pausing for a second, I need to admit something. At this point in my career I knew nothing. I was a green PA. I panicked. I'm not proud of it, but I learned from it.

I immediately picked up my walkie and told the ADs, "The van is across the street from set, but it's blocked in by some police cars and I'm not sure how to get it out." I then do the only thing that I know how to do at this point: I call Locations. I explain that there are squad cars blocking our SWAT van and there are no drivers. I frantically tell them that we need a tow truck or we're not going to have a van for the next scene. This news throws every department into a frantic snit. Nobody knew what was going on or where the van was. This pandemonium continued for about 45 minutes.

Finally an unfamiliar voice breaks through on Channel 1: "Hi, this is the Prop Department. I just wanted to let you folks know that the SWAT van just landed and we're about to start dressing it. FYI, you could have just asked us...." Boy, was my face red. The van I had spotted was a *real* SWAT van! That day I learned: Ask before you assume!

PROPS

Props (short for property) are considered any item that an actor holds, eats, or uses in any way during the course of a scene. Props come from the department with the same name. Aside from the actual props themselves, the Prop (sometimes called Props) Department is also in charge of securing and moving vehicles in the movie (picture cars), maintaining a basic medical kit on-set, and dispensing props to both principal and background actors, as well as setting and moving cast chairs.

● *THE PEOPLE*

The Prop Department is headed by the Property Master. He is responsible for obtaining and/or creating the props on-set. The Assistant Property Master is the person who is actually on-set making sure that everyone has what is needed for the scene. Under this person are the Prop Assistants and the Prop Shopper. The assistants are the ones who will actually be handing out props on-set while the Property Masters are coordinating and prepping items for the next scene. Last but not least, the Prop Shopper does exactly what you would expect... *shops!* He gets to leave set and pick up all of the props or materials that are needed.

● *WORKING WITH PROPS*

The relationship between a PA and the Prop Department can be very delicate. If they like you, don't worry; if they think you're incompetent, be prepared to work hard and ask for things multiple times. One of the biggest mistakes PAs regularly make is moving the cast chairs without permission. While it seems like a simple task, you are not in their union, you cannot do it! Go ahead, try. I guarantee a Prop Representative will chew you out. Now the proper way to do it is to ask a Prop Rep to move the chair. If they say they are too busy, ask permission to move the chair. And when all else fails, get the okay from an AD so when questioned later you have a justifiable reason for your actions.

• THINGS PROPS WILL DO FOR YOU

If you're a Background PA, you should be in contact with Props and give them as much notice as possible so that they have enough time to prop up (give props to) your background. If you are a 1st Team PA or a Key PA, talk to Props about umbrellas and cast chairs for your actors. They will also be responsible for any heaters or fans used to keep the talent comfortable. If you need a quick fix for an arts and crafts project, the Prop Department will have all kinds of creative solutions that will at the very least get you started.

SOUND

The Sound Department is, of course, in charge of the sound, and these folks hear everything. And I mean *everything!* From producers' comments, to background gossip, to actors' day-to-day lives… they are always listening.

• THE EQUIPMENT

The two most common ways of recording sound are:

1) Using a boom (a long pole with a microphone at the end).

2) Using a lavaliere mike (a wireless unit with a hidden microphone), also known as a wire.

© Michelle Pace 2009.

• THE PEOPLE

The Sound Department is responsible for putting the wires on the actors and making sure that everything is heard clearly and cleanly. It usually consists of only three members: the boss, known as the sound mixer, the boom operator, and the utility sound tech. The mixer sits at the sound cart and adjusts the sound levels as the words come from the actors' mouths. He will also help to put the wires on the actors' bodies and control the volume at which they pick up sound. If three actors are wearing microphones in a scene and one of them is talking, the mixer will raise the volume on the actor who is speaking, while shutting off the other two actors who are listening. The boom operator holds the boom pole and follows the actors walking through the scene. He will need to watch all of the rehearsal to plan his path in a way that keeps him out of the camera's view. The utility sound tech listens for unwanted noise from the surrounding areas and keeps track of all of the paperwork, recording which tracks will be used and when. He will also assist in wiring actors when they come to set.

Sometimes the Sound Department will hire a playback technician to be in charge of working a sound board at a club, or controlling music for a scene with a lot of actors in it. The playback technician will have a list of cues so he knows where to stop and start a song while the actors play in the scene.

HOW MANY WIRES?

When dealing with the Sound Department, remember... they have good ears! You won't have to tell them things more than twice and chances are someone else already has. So to deal with this, pose your question like so: "Has anyone asked about wires yet?" Now you're off the hook. You've just asked if they've been asked, so you've saved yourself from being redundant. The answer will either be "Yes," or "No, we'll have to wire...." Remember to find out how many wires will be needed before the actors are called to set to shoot, but after Sound has gotten a chance to see a rehearsal *with camera!* After the rehearsal they will be able to give you a definite answer.

THE ACTORS ARE COMING...

Once you have that answer, don't forget to remind the Sound folks as actors are coming. Let one of the Sound Reps know that the actor is on-set and waiting to be wired: they will take care of the rest. Your job at this point will be to monitor the process. Keep your ADs updated on who's getting wired and how far along they are... or at least be prepared to answer those questions.

Communicating with the Camera

I was working on a movie called *Salt* with seven different cameras. The scene was a vice-presidential funeral parade with a full-on color guard, Secret Service, marching band, CIA, FBI, etc. The entire scene spanned roughly 20 city blocks. I was on "F" camera, which was on a crane in the middle of New York's Park Avenue. My job was to pay attention to the walkie and give instructions to the cameraman on how to frame each shot. This was a massive effort and I was a cog in the gigantic film machine. In this situation I had to convey precisely what the director wanted in a clear way that the cameraman could quickly understand. I didn't tell him to move the camera left: I asked him to pan left and frame up on the motorcade. The more specific terminology you can use, the easier the job will be. Remember that. Say what you mean.

CAMERA

The Camera Department is responsible for the big picture... literally! They operate the cameras, check the focus, and deal with anything that relates to the actual moving image. The Camera Department will build the camera body: It consists of a motorized apparatus, a battery pack, and a lens attachment. They also build the video village. Camera will set up monitors and run cables so that the director can watch the action.

The Camera Department is made up of the Camera Operator, the 1st Assistant Cameraman, the 2nd Assistant Cameraman, and the loader. With all of the new technology and the digital movement in filmmaking, we can now add Digital Imaging Technician (DIT) to the Camera Department's roster. Related to these positions are the Camera PA and the Director of Photography; I'll tell you about them in a moment.

● *THE MEN BEHIND THE LENS — OPERATORS, ACs, LOADERS*

The Camera Operator has the most obviously titled job. He... drumroll, please... operates the camera! But it doesn't stop there: The Camera Operator is the creative eye behind the director. He makes the director's vision come to life through the lens by interpreting the director's instructions. He'll tweak shots for optimum angles and plan the entire scene in his head, shot by shot. The Camera Operator is invaluable to a PA because he will tell you exactly what the shot is and what the camera will be seeing, so that you can pull down parking signs, clear traffic cones, and set the background for the scene. Do this before the ADs ask you to. And don't tell the unions!

The 1st AC is the Camera Operator's right-hand man. He is responsible for checking the focus on the camera and setting the zooms. The operator and the 1st AC work very closely and must be able to read each other well. They are supported by the 2nd AC.

The 2nd AC is the man that you should definitely know. Sometimes called a "marker," the 2nd AC is responsible for putting colored tape (a different color for each actor) on the ground to mark the actors' positions in a scene. The 2nd AC is also in charge of the slate (or clapboard). A description will follow shortly. Along with the above-mentioned tasks, the 2nd AC must also keep track of the takes that are good and the ones that are not going to be used. He writes the scenes, the amount of film used per take as well as the title of the take and which shots will be printed (developed and used). For a PA, the main thing to remember is that when a marking rehearsal begins, the marker and/or the 2nd AC are there and ready.

The loader is the entry-level union job in the Camera Department. The loader exchanges empty mags (film holders on a camera) for ones filled with unexposed film. He takes the mags back to the darkroom and moves the exposed film from the mag into a film canister. He then reloads the mag with new unexposed film and it's ready to go. At the end of the night, the loader will box up all of the film for the day as well as any paperwork that needs to go to the developers. A PA only needs to know that at the end of the night, this is the person you see about picking up the film and dropping it off at a development company.

The DIT is responsible for basic upkeep and maintenance on digital cameras, reviewing footage that has been shot, and transferring footage from camera media cards to hard drives that will later be sent to the editors. He can preview footage and playback clips for the director to critique in about 15 minutes. This is incredible compared to the long process of developing film that usually takes days before a finished product is returned.

● *THE NON-CAMERA CAMERA FOLKS*

Did you know that the Camera PA is technically a member of the Production Department? The union representing camera crew does not recognize the PA as a potential member. The Camera PA is responsible for setting up the video village (a system of monitors that allows the director and producer to watch the scene), getting camera batteries and carrying cable, as well as making sure that all portable monitors are charged. For a Production PA, this means that if the video village needs to move, or you need a monitor, talk to the Camera PA.

The Director of Photography (DP) is responsible for the look, feel, and mood of the light. He takes light readings using a light meter and counts off the f-stop (a measure of light that tells the camera what size the lens aperture should be for optimum light) to the 1st AC, who adjusts the camera accordingly.

The Director of Photography has very little to do with the PAs in general, but always has fantastic stories from set and incredible insights into the industry. Just know who and where the DP is, so that when the 1st AD calls, you can be the one to say, "I've got him/her/it!"

● *THE SLATE*

I promised I'd describe a slate to you, and I didn't want you to wait too long, so there's a drawing of a slate on the next page. It contains all of the information that an editor will need to piece together the film and sync (synchronize, or match up) the sound. It contains the scene number, the take name, the episode title, and it may or may not contain an electronic counter that will sync with the sound mixer's equipment. Depending on the slate, you will also see the date, the show title, the production company, the director's name, the DP's name, the producer's name, etc.

Joshua A. Friedman 2009.

● TYPES OF CAMERA RIGS

Another tidbit of information that every PA should know is the different types of rigs used to shoot a scene. While there are more rigs being built and created all of the time, we typically only use three main rigs: handheld, Steadicam, and dolly.

The handheld camera rig consists of a camera body, a shoulder pad, and two handles that stick out of the front.

Handheld rig

The Steadicam rig is a larger rig broken into two pieces. There is a body piece, which the cameraman will wear around his waist, and a fluid arm extension that holds the camera steady and level for a smooth moving shot.

Steadicam rig

Last comes the dolly. The dolly is a cart that holds the camera and the cameraman. It can be used as both a tripod and as a moving platform. It has an arm that extends to raise or lower the camera depending on

Dolly
© *Dan Brosnan 2009.*

the angle required. The dolly is great for tracking shots or slight movements in a small space.

Now that you have a broad overview of the Camera Department, let's examine the elements that will shape the picture.

ELECTRICS & GRIPS

• ELECTRICS

The electrics (electricians, but always called electrics on-set) are in charge of supplying the entire set with power. They run thousands of feet of cable over the set, put the lights up on the stands (called hi-boys or low-boys depending on the height), and make sure that everything is running properly. In addition to this, they also cut gels (transparent colored plastic). Gels and diffusions are used to change the temperature and intensity of a light. In general, you could say that electrics put light on the set and adjust the color and intensity (how bright or dim the light will be). The Electric Department consists of the gaffer (so named for a large stick called a gaff hook that was once used to adjust the light's intensity), the Best Boy, the lamp operators, and the genny (electrical generator) operator.

• ELECTRICAL PEOPLE — CHARGED PERSONALITIES

The gaffer is the head of the department. He helps to translate the DP's vision onto the set. The gaffer communicates to the Best Boy which lights will be needed and oversees the process. It is the Best Boy's job to facilitate the setup of the lights and set the light intensity to the gaffer and the DP's specifications. The lamp operators are the equivalent of electric grips. These are the people who carry the cable, lift the lights, and do all the dirty work that makes each shot so brilliantly beautiful. Genny operators have a great job. They are required to stay by their generator, set it up, keep it working, and break it down at the end of the night. The genny operator is incredibly important because without this guy, nobody on-set would have any power. The monitors would be dead, the dolly wouldn't charge, and you'd be using flashlights and candles.

● *LET THERE BE LIGHT*

Electrics not only put light on the set, they also provide light for the entire crew. They make dark hallways safer, light the bathrooms and the Crafty (food service) table, and keep lights by all the trucks when shooting at night so crewmembers can see what they are working on.

● *WHO SHOULD I TALK TO?*

The only thing you'll need to focus on as a PA is the Best Boy and maybe the gaffer. If you need an electric, call for the Best Boy and he'll delegate the responsibility to his crew.

As a general rule, ask the Best Boy for what is needed. You are not the boss of the crewmembers just because you need something done. Go through the proper channels efficiently, and know whom you will need to talk with to get things done.

● *GRIPS*

If you want a one-sentence description of the Grip Department: They shape the light. The Director of Photography will tell a grip to throw up a black or a diffusion (types of flags) to soften or bounce the light onto an actor. You'll know the grips because they are the folks that look like they'll take you out. Grips are the folks that do the lugging, the setting, the leveling, etc., on-set. They have to be strong because all day long they are doing manual labor.

● *HOW DID GRIPS GET THEIR NAME?*

A scenic artist I once worked with explained to me that grips were named after the tool bags that they carried. The tool bags were soft-sided and heavy with a soft grip to make them easier to carry. Since they always had these on their person, the name grip stuck. There are four main jobs in the Grip Department that every PA should know.

● *THE GRIP PEOPLE*

The Key Grip is the person in charge. He goes on the scouts, he listens to the director and the DP, and when something is needed, he's immediately on his walkie-talkie calling for things to happen.

Under the Key Grip is the Best Boy. He will handle the hiring of the crew and help keep everything organized on the truck. While the Key Grip is calling on the walkie, the grips are answering. They are some of the hardest workers I know. Please understand… they may not be in a good mood. They just dragged 300 pounds of sandbags across the set and then were told to move them back to the original position. Now you, the PA, are asking them to move their equipment. Good luck! Be nice (as you should always be to every department), find an opportune moment to let the grips know what you need, and choose whom you will speak to. Tell the Key Grip or Best Boy what you need and who asked for it. He'll take care of the rest. The dolly grip is the fourth type of grip that I will discuss. The dolly grip handles everything related to the dolly. He helps build and set the track, builds the dolly up, charges the power supply, and finesses the dolly down the track to create the camera move for each shot. The dolly grip has little to do with your work as a PA. Just know who he is in case someone calls.

● *WHAT GRIPS DO*

If electrics throw light onto a set, grips take the light off. They bounce, shape, and soften light using fabric-wrapped frames called flags. Flags come in all shapes and sizes and are made of multiple materials. Black flags are wrapped in solid Duvetyn (a strong, soft, light linen-like fabric) and meant to stop or block the light on-set. Diffusion gels are set in frames and help soften the light on-set. White board is used to bounce light. The grips are responsible for moving any heavy equipment, any type of construction job (when construction is not available), laying dolly track, building the dolly, setting C-stands (stands used to hold flags), and more.

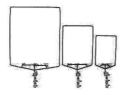

Flags and a C-stand. © *Michelle Pace 2009.*

SCENIC

The Scenic is an on-set artist who can pretty much make anything imaginable. If the director feels that something is too reflective or shiny, props need to be aged, or a wall needs to be patched, painted, and retouched, the Scenic is who you go to. She can make anything look new or different.

● *PRESENT THE PROBLEM, NOT THE SOLUTION*

A common mistake that most PAs and ADs make is to tell the Scenic what they'll need to bring to set. For example, "Paul, can you come in with some dulling spray to take down a shiny door-knob?" You shouldn't do this because you may be wrong. Suppose the doorknob will be turned by an actor. Dulling spray may not be the best solution. The Scenic will usually know what's needed and have other options available. To avoid this problem, you should always tell the Scenic what you need done and let them decide which tools should be used.

● *BE PATIENT*

Remember, some things take time. Give the Scenic as much notice as you can so she is not running frantically to satisfy your request. More often than not a problem is discovered on-set during a camera rehearsal. The Scenic is called in to solve the problem and must have everything finished, dried, and ready for the scene by the time the actors come to set. For a Scenic, time is always of the essence.

SET DRESSING

The variations of set dressers can be separated into two groups. The first are simply called set dressers.

● *SET DRESSERS*

They come in before you even get to set. These dressers will stick the kid's toys in a pile in the middle of the floor, and then smash the place to hell because the script says "a ransacked living room with child's toys strewn about." As a PA you will rarely deal with these people. Like a lot of the info I've given you, it's just so you are aware of the facts.

This is a fake subway used by the setdressers on *Law & Order: Criminal Intent*. © *Joshua A. Friedman 2009*.

I spent most of my night preventing drunk New Yorkers from trying to enter! © *Joshua A. Friedman 2009*.

● *ON-SET DRESSER*

The on-set dressers will be your go-to people when you are actually on-set. To clarify, any item on-set that is not considered a prop is considered set dressing. These folks do everything from adjusting lamps to reduce camera glare, to changing clocks and moving furniture. If a window or door is causing a lens flare in the camera, the on-set dresser will correct the problem. If you need a chair (not a cast chair) or a stool, you tell the on-set dressers. If crime-scene tape needs to be put up, you call the on-set dressers.

The ADs will constantly ask for things that involve the on-set dressers. Know who they are and be prepared to ask them for what you need.

Scripty Style

The Script Supervisor sits next to the top dogs. He/she hears everything that goes on. I was working with a director on the show *Gossip Girl* who I felt was moving incredibly slowly. He would set up a shot, shoot it once, and then change it completely. And as he was about to shoot it again... he'd change something else. I felt that this made him a bad director. To me he was shooting a TV show like a feature film, spending a lot of money and assuming he had a lot of time. I mentioned my feelings to the Script Supervisor and she had to disagree with me.

She sat next to the producers and heard all of their likes and dislikes with the day's work. He was moving very slowly, yes, but what I did not see was the end result. This particular episode of the show was very important so the producers were more willing to let the director take his time. The Script Supervisor explained the art and the aesthetic eye that this particular director was using. I learned a lot about directing through conversations like that and I've also started to hone my personal aesthetic eye.

SCRIPT SUPERVISOR

The Script Supervisor (nicknamed Scripty) is the head of his/her department. I was once told by one of my favorite Script Supervisors that, "I am a department of one. When the company moves, I don't have helpers. It's just me." Offer some assistance when you have the time. It will not go unnoticed and will help you build a relationship.

● SCRIPTY DOES WHAT?

The job of a Script Supervisor is to follow along with the script as scenes are being shot. She keeps track of what is being said and makes notes that will go to the editor at the end of the day. Scripty also looks for continuity errors from shot to shot, corrects line readings, and times out scenes. The Script Supervisor will mark down any mistakes during the scene as well as a description of each shot, and the take number.

● BE SURE TO PASS THE MESSAGE

The job is difficult and requires a lot of focus and concentration. It also involves a lot of communication. Scripty sits at the video village next to the director. Usually the village is at a distance from set. Because of this, a PA should always be stationed near the village to facilitate communication between Scripty and the set. You will tell Scripty information you hear over the walkie, such as, "This shot will be tight over Dave's shoulder onto Emily." Scripty will then give you a slate name for the Camera Department.

● READING THE SLATE

Scenes are slated (labeled) using scene numbers. Setups (every time the camera frame changes is considered a new setup) are slated using the phonetic alphabet (A = Apple, B = Baker, C = Charlie, etc.). The first setup is slated simply with the scene number and the take number. Each additional setup will be labeled using the alphabet. And takes are slated using numbers. When you combine all of this information in the following example, you will understand how to read a slate.

If Scripty calls out "Scene 68, Baker, Take 4," you will know that this is the fourth take of the third setup in scene 68.

● SCRIPTY — THE TIMEKEEPER

Besides keeping track of the scenes and takes, Scripty will let a PA know what time the first shot of the day rolled as well as what time the first shot after lunch rolled. Essentially, Scripty is the official timekeeper on-set. When questions arise from the shop steward (the person representing the unions on the job), you will always defer time issues to the Script Supervisor's clock. At the end of the day the final thing that a PA needs to get is the official camera wrap from the Script Supervisor.

● WHEN TO COMMUNICATE

Most of this information is for the Paperwork PA, but if you have it, you'll be able to help more on-set. Please remember your place in the hierarchy. If you are an additional PA, this stuff is already taken care of. If you are a staff PA, be sure to double-check with your team so multiple people don't bother the Script Supervisor. At this point, just be aware.

CRAFT SERVICES

Craft services is the department that makes the crew very happy. How do they make the crew happy? FOOD! Craft services is responsible for the health and happiness of the crew. Bad food will be the next big thing at the water cooler, so make sure you have a steady supply of food that the crew likes. Snacks as well as fresh fruit and vegetables. Sandwiches are usually a good bet. Along with the normal snack foods and a steady supply of sodas, juices, and water, Crafty makes hot meals throughout the day. The hot meals will usually arrive on-set roughly four hours after crew call, then again three to four hours after lunch. In between they are constantly restocking everything else on the Crafty table.

Crafty Knows Best

As a PA you are asked to do all kinds of fun and not-so-fun things. One of these things is food runs/orders. When I was working on *Gossip Girl* I had a delightful experience with one of the actors on the show. She had requested a breakfast fruit and yogurt with some juice. I grabbed all of the requested items, a napkin, a fork, and headed back to the actress. When I gave her the yogurt it hit me... *spoon!* She was gracious, calm. I told her I'd run back and get her one. And she replied that I should just get back to work, she'll eat her yogurt with a fork. It was a great experience with what could have been a disastrous situation. On the flip side to this was another experience.

On a TV show that shall remain nameless, I was getting an actor coffee one day. It was my first time taking a crack at the chore and this actor liked his coffee a certain way. I make it and bring it to him on-set. Too dark. He knocks the coffee out of my hand sending it onto me and the set. He likes his coffee caramel, like the color of cardboard. So I made the coffee again. The right color this time and all was fine. Here's how this relates to Crafty (the craft service person).

If you get to know Crafty, ask for his or her help: They'll know exactly what everyone on the crew likes to eat and how they like their food prepared. This goes for coffee, sandwiches, specialty items, etc. Crafty will know and it will help you to take better care of the production team.

● *HOT FOOD*

When hot food arrives on-set you should write down the menu and be prepared to take orders from producers, directors, and ADs. It's a great way to network and the crewmembers will love you for it. My personal favorite is hot chocolate-chip cookies. The second these delectable treats hit the Crafty table I snatch up the tray and some napkins and offer them to all the crewmembers. Now they all remember my name and are more willing to work with me, because I help make them happy. A side note to bringing food to set: Make sure that you bring everything that will be needed to eat that food (forks, knives, spoons, napkins, etc.). There's nothing worse than a PA who brings the director a sloppy joe and no napkin. So, again: Be prepared.

We Don't Do Coffee

I was working on a gig once where the 2nd AD asked me to get coffee for the production staff. She gives me the order and tells me to call Transpo (Transportation) and ask for a van. So I turn my walkie to the Teamster channel, identify myself and say, "Do you have a van available for a coffee run?" Nothing but crickets (dead air... you can run a train through the space).

I tried to get in touch with the Teamsters again. I picked up my walkie and said, "Josh for Transpo...."

They respond, "Go for Transpo."

"Hey guys, I was asked to go on a coffee run, do you have a van available?"

I wait and hear: "We don't do coffee." I thought he was messing with me so I walk to a van, tap on the window, and tell the driver that the ADs sent me on a coffee run. He radios the Teamster Captain who says, "We don't do coffee."

Part of being a PA is being resourceful. With my options dwindling and the Teamsters unwilling to assist me, I was forced to seek an alternate method of getting the job done. In this situation, I ended up running two miles up the road to a coffee shop and running back. When faced with a challenge, I found a solution, no matter what it took.

TRANSPO

The Transportation Department (Transpo) is made up of the International Brotherhood of Teamsters. Make friends with them. Teamsters do all of the driving on-set. They are charged with the care and maintenance of the base camp vehicles, the working trucks (camera, props, grip, electric), and the 15 passenger vans.

• THE PEOPLE

Two people usually head Transpo, a transportation captain and a co-captain. The captain finds a central location and acts as a dispatcher for all the vans. Under these two captains are a team of truck drivers and van drivers who do miraculous things for production. There will be one driver for every working truck, and sometimes an extra for maintenance or repairs. Besides the working trucks, a captain will hire at least one van driver to pick up actors, equipment, and crewmembers.

• LEARN FROM THESE MEN, THEY'VE BEEN AROUND

For a PA, one of the best things you can do is get to know the Teamsters. They have invaluable stories and experiences and can really help you along on your path. Make sure you know which driver is assigned to which truck. If you need a van, call the captain and ask if he has anything available. Tell him exactly what the van will be used for. He'll help you when he can. Make sure when you get on the Teamster walkie channel that you identify yourself. If you don't, a response may be a long time coming.

• IN SHORT

The job of the Transportation Department is to move the actors, directors, and crew to and from set as well as transporting any equipment that will be needed for the shooting day.

THE PRODUCTION OFFICE

Production involves a group of individuals working together to create a collaborative project. While the PAs on-set facilitate the technical aspects of production, there is a whole other world associated with logistics in the office.

The production office handles the day-to-day running of the project. Its members include production office staff, accounting staff, the Art Department, the transportation captain, and the above-the-line (ATL, i.e., salaried) employees, such as producers, directors, etc. These departments and individuals work in the office every day, planning, coordinating, and communicating with everyone involved with the project. This is home base. Grand Central, Ground Zero for every job. If every department were a planet, this office would be the sun. And it all starts in production.

PRODUCTION DEPARTMENT (OFFICE)

In the office, the Production Department rules the roost. The members of this department perform any number of tasks including, but not limited to, arranging travel, tracking down supplies, negotiating with vendors, and dealing with any number of logistical needs associated with the project. Anything that is needed on-set must first be examined and inventoried by the production office. The office keeps a log of all packages, purchase orders, script revisions, and any other paperwork that may be needed as reference material at any point during production. If an accident occurs on-set, the office files the claim with an insurance company and follows up afterwards.

Throughout the shooting day the office will report on the status of production to the studio or producing company behind the project. They will tell the studio what time shooting began that day, when the company broke for lunch, and what time production wrapped for the day. If necessary, they may field questions about employee travel arrangements and film stock inventories (how much film is being shot each day).

As the center of production, all mail stops through the production office. They receive everything from bills to actors' personal

Welcome to the Fortress

A production office often doubles as a production storage space. It houses everything from equipment and food to costumes and supplies. Due to the value of the stored items (including the cash from accounting), the office tends to become an almost impenetrable fortress.

I was working in one such fortress on a job in the middle of January. Now for any New Yorkers reading this, you know... IT'S COLD! To enter this particular fortress required a six-step security process involving five different keys and a code. I pull up to the building at about three o'clock in the morning. Here's how it went down....

- Key 1 opens the padlock on the sliding gate to the driveway.
- Key 2 opens the padlock on the liftgate control box.
- Key 3 controls the gate itself. The gate slides up to reveal a glass front door to the building.
- Key 4 opens the front door allowing access to the building, but not before setting off the alarm.
- Enter Alarm code and disarm within thirty seconds.... Phew!
- Key 5 opens the front door of the physical production office.

On this particular night the temperature was in the teens. I stuck my key in lock 1 and had no problem. The gate opened and I moved onto the liftgate control box. Insert key... nothing. Twist key... nothing. I twist one more time, bracing my foot against the building and pulling as hard as I can, but to no avail. The fortress has won.

But I'm a PA, right? Resourceful is my middle name. I walked around to the back of the building and found an unlocked window, which of course set off the alarm as I climbed through. I turned off the alarm and finished my paperwork for the day.

Now the tricky part. Because of the gate I had to go back the way I came in. This included resetting the alarm. I walked my path from the code box to the window, propped open all of the doors with easily movable items (trashcans, fake plants, and folding chairs) and braced myself for the challenge. I put in the code and booked it to the window, kicking away my doorstops as I went so it looked like I was never there. Once through the window, a feeling of pride came over me. I did it... and I didn't get caught!

The next night I find a note by the liftgate along with a hammer and an empty blowtorch. The note read, "Saw the security footage.... Just in case...."

Welcome to the Fortress.

mail and producers' luggage. The mail is very important, as it may contain scripts, revisions, contracts, or any number of time-sensitive materials. The office ensures that the packages and mail get to where they need to be and fast.

Besides mail, the office will distribute copies of scripts, schedules, and memos to all appropriate parties using a distribution (distro) list. The distro list is simply a list of names divided up by department. Next to each department heading is a number that indicates how many copies will be needed. Below the heading are the names of the crew-members who will receive copies. After all copies have been made, or concurrently for efficiency's sake, a PA must write the first initial and last name of the recipient in the top right corner. All copies are grouped by department and placed in the "To Set" box for distribution.

THE OFFICE HIERARCHY

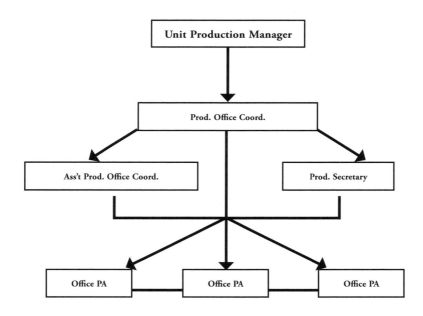

We've established the purpose of the production office. Now it's time to dig a little deeper and examine the players.

THE PEOPLE

The person in charge of putting the office together is called the production office coordinator (POC). The POC wears many, many hats. He hires the rest of the office staff and with them will organize payments, pickups and drop-offs of supplies, etc. He is the person who spends the most time on the phone communicating with the studio or the producing company attached to the project. If necessary the POC will also make calls to vendors and other crew-members. In short, the POC manages every aspect of the office. To assist in these duties, the POC hires an assistant production office coordinator (APOC). The APOC assists the POC during the day, and stays late to cover him at night. He will be responsible for making any required corrections to the production report before it is approved. While the APOC is assisting the POC, who will answer the phone? The last member of our three-headed office government is the production secretary. Her main concerns are ordering sup-plies, answering the phones, and most importantly, facilitating the lunch order. Together, these three individuals make a great team that can really help keep production on track.

Aside from these three figureheads, there are usually two or three PAs who help man the phones, make copies, and go on runs. These are the Office PAs. An Office PA can be compared to an everyday additional PA on-set. They are hired to standby until something is needed and hopefully learn a few things in the process. Regardless of what the office has you doing, it's a great way to get your feet wet.

PRODUCTION OFFICE COORDINATOR

The POC is considered the captain of the office vessel. He com-municates with the mainland (set) and follows orders quickly and efficiently. The POC arranges the schedule of runs and pickups for the day. This list of tasks is generated through meetings and phone calls with producers and department heads. During these meetings a POC will ask what equipment will be needed, what dates it will be needed for, and who he should talk to at the venue. Equipment can be anything from replacement parts and tape stock to lifts, cranes, and extra generators. The POC must always stay ahead of the production schedule so that all equipment that will be needed is ordered in advance. Along with the scheduling of these runs, something always happens on-set that requires a special run. You never know what might be needed, so look out. It may be an interesting challenge.

● CONTRACTS

One of the main responsibilities of a POC is to draw up actor contracts and send them to set. In conjunction with the UPM, the ADs, and the first team PA, the POC will type up the contract and send it to set to be signed and returned. Along with actor contracts, the POC will deal with vendor contracts during the production.

● VENDORS & PURCHASE ORDERS

A large part of the POC's job involves their relationships with vendors. A vendor is any company that provides a service or product for the production. When a POC and a vendor are on good terms, they will be able to expedite orders, throw in small favors, even apply discounts to equipment package rentals. Once a deal is struck, the POC will fill out a purchase order (PO) containing the following information:
- Purchase order number
- Name and address of purchaser
- Name and address of vendor
- Date of purchase
- Item number and description of purchase
- Price per unit, number of units, and total cost before taxes
- Shipping method
- Payment method
- Tax (though you should be exempt) and shipping fees
- Grand total
- Signature of applicable parties for approval

Every PO must be approved by the UPM and properly filed for future reference. An example of a purchase order can be found in Appendix C of this book.

● *TRAVEL*

The POC may be asked to not only work with the vendors, but also to act as travel agent to production's visitors. They will find accommodations for actors and producers while at the same time providing a detailed and well-researched list of services and sites in the area. It takes a lot of planning and coordination; that's why you hire an APOC!

ASSISTANT PRODUCTION OFFICE COORDINATOR

The APOC's job will differ from project to project. As the right-hand man of the POC, the APOC will often be responsible for overseeing a specific area. Some APOCs track and arrange all travel for production, some correct production reports, and still others will organize and handle purchase orders. APOCs specialize where they are most needed by the POC. Along with their assigned tasks, APOCs are responsible for a few other things. They assist in the "day filing" of paperwork. This means they help organize, copy, and store all of the paperwork from set (PRs, Exhibit Gs, call sheets, etc,) for future reference.

● *THE MESSAGE*

Most APOCs will leave the nightly message on the production answering machine. It will go something like this:

"Hello, you've reached the _____ production office. Call times for (date) are (time). Business hours are from (time) until (time). If you'd like to leave a message, we will get back to you as soon as possible. Thank you and have a great week."

Sometimes they'll be funnier, sometimes more dry, but you get the gist.

Whatever the assigned task, the APOC is there to help and can be an excellent resource when you have questions.

When you talk with the office on a regular basis, you learn that the person whom you need an answer from is not necessarily the person you should talk to first. Many times when I have a question for the POC he is busy or on the phone. I then defer to the APOC, who is sometimes also busy and on the phone. So I move down the line to the production secretary.

PRODUCTION SECRETARY

The secretary's voice is most likely the first one you'll hear when calling the office. She answers the phones, facilitates and assists in the morning copy and filing rituals, and tracks the logging of packages that move through the office.

● ORDERING SUPPLIES

The most important aspect of the secretary's job (at least from a PA's perspective) is that she will order all of your supplies. The secretary puts in the orders for most of the expendables that you will need. These can range from office supplies to medicine and hand warmers. Remember to think ahead and order things in advance. It's harder to get warmers on-set when it's twenty degrees outside and all the shops have sold out.

In the paperwork section we discussed giving your supply list to the production secretary. Make sure that your list is precise. List the exact products that you would like with item/reference numbers associated. Search through the supply catalog with your ADs and ask what their preferences are on pens, pencils, etc. It's a fun bonding experience if you know what you like. Once you've figured out what you will need, type up your list in an easy-to-read spreadsheet, print it, and hand it to the secretary. Email it too, as a backup, and don't forget to follow up if you're missing any supplies. If you're out of toner, someone will want to know why.

OFFICE PA

Aside from the top three, the office is home to two or three PAs. These PAs are responsible for answering the phones, making copies and filing, and going on the different runs scheduled throughout the day. The three most important runs of the day are (in no particular order) the breakfast run, the morning coffee run, and the editorial run. Didn't see the third one coming, did you? Editorial is important because this is the place where production will receive the dailies for viewing.

A Day in the Life of an Office PA

I interviewed an Office PA who described a typical day in the office on the movie *It's Kind of a Funny Story*. Here's her firsthand account of a typical day:

"The first shift comes into the office around 8:00 a.m. and checks the messages left over from the night before."

There are two shifts in the office. An early shift that goes home between 6:00 p.m. and 8:00 p.m., and a later shift that goes home once the camera has wrapped on-set. The schedules regarding these shifts are determined by the POC.

"After we check the messages, we make copies of the daily paperwork. Each copy is labeled and grouped for an individual or a department before being distributed in the office or on-set."

PAs know how many copies to make using distro lists. As each copy is made and accounted for, the PA will check off a box next to the names and departments on the distro list. The check indicates that the distro was copied and delivered.

Typically, a production office will receive four or five different deliveries during the course of the day. When a package arrives, it must be logged into the package log before moving on to its final destination.

The package log is a list that contains all of the information needed to track a package from arrival to delivery. The log will tell the office the dates and times a package arrived, who it was sent from, who it was sent to, and what the contents are. This system makes it easier to track down packages when they go missing between the office and set.

"Lunch in the office starts around 10:00 a.m. We pick two different restaurants and pass menus around the office. Along with the menus we pass around an order sheet or two for each restaurant. Employees fill out their name, their order, and the price, and pass it along. Once all the orders have been collected, it's time to call them in. I have yet to have a perfect order. Don't fret, people are used to this. But do try to make the orders right. Be patient with the people on the phone, you have a big order, and they'll be the ones handling your food. After lunch the POC will create a to-do list for the later shift. Now the afternoon begins."

It's important to note that while managing the above tasks, the Office PAs will also be answering the phone, copying, filing, and running around town on any number of errands. Usually the number of runs will increase as the day goes on.

"The afternoon is filled with more of the same from the morning, but businesses are in full swing during these hours so we tend to go on more runs. We pick up and deliver film, cases, and supplies for every department. Sometimes we'll have to run to an actor's residence to retrieve a forgotten script, wardrobe, or medication. The runs will keep us busy until shops close. Then we just wait for wrap.

At wrap, we copy and distribute the call sheet and create the sides for the following day."

The sides are $8\frac{1}{2}''$ x $5\frac{1}{2}''$ copies of the script pages that will be shot during the day. The first page is always a miniature copy of the call sheet with the script pages for the screen required stapled in chronological order behind them.

"After the sides are copied, stapled, and cut, we will group them into stacks and leave them for the Paperwork PA to take to set. We then leave the nightly message on the office answering machine and lock all of the office doors. If we're on our way home before 11:00 p.m. it's usually a good night".

THE ON-SET EXPERIENCE

Anticipating the Process

If you know the process you can anticipate what will be needed and what happens next. I was working on a movie called 13 with a very popular movie star in New York. We were shooting two scenes consecutively and I had to get an actor (let's call him John) ready in Hair and Makeup for the second scene only. The other two actors I had on-set were needed for both scenes and ready to go. I knew that the assistant directors wanted all of the actors on-set by the time they began shooting the first of the two scenes. I got John back to the Hair and Makeup trailer while the crew worked with the 2nd Team. Once he was ready, I put him in a van and sent him straight to set to wait with the director. The director sees John and flips out! He doesn't like his mustache. He sends John back to Hair and Makeup. This process happens three more times: By the last time, the crew had completed the first scene and I was getting down to the wire. I had about five minutes to get this actor to set for a marking rehearsal. His mustache was finally perfect and he had to make a personal phone call.... Because I knew our situation on-set I called the ADs and asked for a little favor. "Can you use the 2nd Teamer for the marking rehearsal, because John has been in and out of this Hair chair for the last hour and a half and needs a personal moment?" Of course the answer was yes and everything worked out. As the marking rehearsal ended, John pulled up fresh and ready to give it a go. If I hadn't known the process, I would not have been able to cover my friends on-set when I ran out of time back at base camp.

WORKING ON-SET

Now that we know who the production players are and what their respective jobs entail, we can examine the actual process on-set. It is routine, repetitive, and sometimes tedious, but everything is done for a reason. Below you will find a simplified shooting process used on most film sets.

- Reading the Words
- Private Director's Rehearsal
- Marking Rehearsal
- 2nd Team/Background Rehearsal
- 1st-Team Rehearsal
- Last Looks
- Shooting

THE REHEARSAL PROCESS

READING THE WORDS

The first part of the process is relatively simple. The principal actors come to set and sit with the director to read the script. Your job is to make sure that the actors and director have a quiet, comfortable working space. Anyone who is not needed should be asked to leave this rehearsal.

PRIVATE DIRECTOR'S REHEARSAL

After this read-through will be another rehearsal for the principal actors, this time with blocking (movement) so they can rehearse their motions. Again, only the key players (director, actors, 1st AD, Director of Photography, camera operators) should be present.

MARKING REHEARSAL

The next rehearsal is called a marking rehearsal. Everyone watches this rehearsal so they will know what is going on in the scene and can do their jobs accordingly. As a PA, you want to make sure that the stand-ins and the marker (camera person with rolls of tape) are close by for this rehearsal.

2nd TEAM/BACKGROUND REHEARSAL

As soon as the marking rehearsal is over, the principal actors will step back to their trailers to change into their wardrobe and get ready to shoot. When this happens, the stand-ins step in so that the grips and electrics can light and the cameraman can rehearse his moves.

1st-TEAM REHEARSAL

If the shot has no dialogue, the principal actors will come back to set and shoot. If the shot is dialogue specific (it has audible lines), then the actors may rehearse one last time. During this rehearsal, the background actors are layered into the scene and positioned to create the reality of the film world.

LAST LOOKS

At this point the 1st AD will call in the Hair, Makeup, and Wardrobe departments for "last looks." And finally! We are ready to shoot.

SHOOTING

Once all of the rehearsals and last looks are done, it is time to roll the cameras. At this stage of the process, everything should be standing by to go, all lockups should be in place, and the set should be completely silent. The 1st AD will call out "roll sound" and the PAs will repeat it for the crew to hear. They shoot and shoot and shoot, and when they are done shooting, the 1st Assistant Cameraman will check the gate (shine a light in the camera aperture to check for dust specks or hairs). If he says, "Good gate," then they move on to the next shot. If the gate is bad… they shoot it one more time.

WALKIE ETIQUETTE

There are a few things you should know about walkies when you enter a set. Everything is simple and basic. Follow these instructions and adapt them to your particular production.

The No. 1 rule on the walkie: Make sure you say *copy!* Listen to everything that is said and copy when appropriate. This lets everyone know that 1) you're there, and 2) you understand what is going on.

Try not to monopolize the walkie channel. Why say with five words what you can say with two? This job is all about efficiency and the walkie is no exception. Here are a few terms that you should know when speaking on the walkie:

#1 — The first principal actor on the call sheet

#2 — The second principal actor on the call sheet

86 — "Forget it."

Abby — Second-to-last shot of the night

Back to 1 — You've finished your conversation on another channel and are switching back to Channel 1.

Bogie — A pedestrian is in the shot.

Breaker, Breaker — Someone is babbling on the walkie and you need to interrupt for something important.

Copy — "I understand."

Cueing — This means that the walkie button is stuck in the talk position and the entire crew can hear everything you said about your warts.

Cut — "The camera cut, it's okay to talk."

Final Touches — "Bring in the Hair, Makeup, and Wardrobe departments."

Flying In... — "I'm coming your way quickly."

Go to (channel #) — "Switch to walkie channel (#)."

Hold the Work — "Stop the working around set, we're trying to shoot."

Kill That... — "Shut it off, shut it down. Stop whatever is happening that shouldn't be."

Last Looks — The last chance Hair, Makeup, and Wardrobe will have to check the actors before the camera rolls. See also *Final Touches.*

Lookie Loo — See *Bogie.*

Looking — If someone is needed, we (the PAs) are searching for them.

Martini — Last shot of the night.

On (channel #) — Let someone know you've switched channels and are listening.

On the Day — While the camera is rolling. For example: "Lockup the sidewalk on the day."

Rehearsal's Up — "Settle in and quiet down, we're about to shoot."

Rolling — "The camera is filming, be quiet."

Standby — "I am busy right now, I'll get back to you in a second."

Steppage — That means you are talking while someone else is talking. Nothing came through clearly on the walkie, so nobody heard you.

Ten-C — A newly coined term for smoking a cigarette (which a lot of actors and directors will step out to do).

Ten-1 (or Ten-2) — A term describing a bathroom break: Ten-1 being a short break and Ten-2 a longer one.

That's a Wrap! — "It's time to go home (almost)."

What's Your 20 — "Where are you?"

The lingo will change from set to set and region to region. But the basics here will get you through what you'll need on your first day.

CALLING IT OUT

A PA once told me "You earn your money with your legs and your lungs." This means move fast and speak loudly. Part of your job is to facilitate communication. This means that when a message needs to be passed on to all of the departments involved in shooting, the PAs are the ones passing it on. To "Call it out," you will simply need to listen to what is being said and repeat aloud the things that the crew needs to hear. One rule that we live by is, "If it's not said on walkie... it isn't said." So if the director yells "Cut," but the AD has not repeated it on the walkie, we consider the camera to still be rolling. Calling things out is also important for crew safety. If a car is backing up, make sure to yell out to the crew, "Car backing up," in order to keep them safe and make everyone aware. Here is a list of the most common things that you will call out:

• Car backing up
• Car coming through, watch your backs (when a street is live and crew is working close to traffic)
• Cut
• Here we go (you'll say this one a lot)
• Quietly, please
• Last looks
• Rolling
• Settling in, please (calm down...)
• Standing by
• While looking for crewmembers, feel free to call out their names.

One Disastrous Night

I was working in SoHo (south of Houston in NYC) on the TV show *Law & Order: Criminal Intent* when an interesting thing happened. At one o'clock in the morning a garbage truck showed up to pick up the trash on our block. We were shooting a scene with stunt cars and had already established the look of the street. The sanitation workers angrily yelled at me for not letting them do their job. The situation escalated to the point of them threatening to beat me up if I didn't let them through. I called the Locations Department to come negotiate the situation.

While this was happening, there was a rave starting on the opposite end of the block. Seven hundred people had been invited to an all-night party. Again, Locations stepped in and helped guide the crowd away from our set. They helped direct traffic. While Locations was attempting to redirect the people, the Lockup PAs were having a hard time stopping the drunk people from plowing into the set. They just didn't understand the words, "Please go around." At least Locations convinced the ravers to close the windows and keep the noise inside.

Back on my end of the block a woman from the building across the street joined the side of the sanitation workers. She complained about the smell of diesel fuel wafting through her window from our condor (a movable platform used to raise lights high in the air).

As our Location Manager negotiated with both parties, the woman ran inside her apartment and called the Fire Department. Six fire trucks entered the middle of our camera shot and stopped to check the problem. The firemen spoke with our Locations Manager and they just laughed. They were used to these situations. The fire trucks created a small diversion, so we backed the garbage truck into our set (after making it wait about two hours) to collect the trash. With the garbage gone and the fire trucks cleared out, we went right back to shooting — until 4:23 a.m. when the hard rain shut us down for good. Hey, it happens. Nothing Locations can do about this one.

LOCKUPS

A good PA knows how to hold a strong lockup. We discussed lock-ups briefly earlier, but let's go into more detail.

STREET LOCKUPS

When locking up a street or sidewalk it is your job to stop people from entering the shot. If the Key PA asks for a hard lock, that means that nobody should get past you. And it does happen: One time I took a punch to the face and an elbow from a homeless man. If someone does get past you, it's not the end of the world. Get on your walkie and say, "Bogie coming through." At all times remember to accept responsibility for the things that you do. If you are not hard locking something, then you are locking up "on the day." "On the day" means while the cameras are shooting. As soon as the director yells "cut" and everything is safe, the Key PA will give the command to release the lockup until the next take. Now a third alternative on a busy street is "letting it live." This means that you are stopping people from staring at the camera while they're on the screen, but at the same time you're not stopping anyone from walking into the shot. It's a great way to get free background.

TRAFFIC LOCKUPS

Another kind of lockup involves traffic and is called a traffic lockup. In order to lockup a street and stop traffic, you must have a TCD (Traffic Control Department) officer with you to stop traffic. Locations are the liaisons between TCD and the production, so, again: Remember to get in good with all of these people.

FIRE WATCH

At some point, you will encounter equipment lockups, the most common of which is known as a fire watch. I don't know where the term comes from, but I do know that you should not take this literally. There is no fire to watch! A fire watch is simply a way for the departments to feel safe and comfortable stepping away from their equipment during lunch. While the crew is away, a PA will sit and keep eyes on the equipment and sometimes a hot set (a set that is dressed and still in use) to ensure that nothing walks away or gets stolen.

Dealing with Celebrity

On a bright sunny day, with a slight wind whipping through the air, I found myself at a middle school in Yonkers, New York, on the set of *The Oranges*. As the actors were in place and the cameras were ready to go, a crew of six schoolchildren showed up to see our star and the cool thing happening on their stomping ground. They were kids, no older than 11 or 12. And they were loud. You remember how you were at that age: obnoxious, inquisitive, rebellious. And always where you were not supposed to be. These kids wormed their way right behind the monitors and began screaming and giggling in the producer's ears. The 2nd 2nd AD approached me and said, "Quiet 'em down or get these kids out of here." I had my Mission.

I approached the children as their eyes grew wide with excitement. They were about to get some attention! The second I was within earshot they started firing off questions:

"What's going on?" "Who is she (the actress)?" "Are you a producer?"

I replied calmly and lured them away from the producers with answers.

"It's a movie called *The Oranges*. I'm a production assistant, not a producer."

They followed me all the way around the corner and continued shouting questions until I refused to answer, waiting for silence. You've got to play the game.

Once the kids calmed down, they realized there was an opportunity to watch. They stood within view of the actress and the cameras, but far enough away that they weren't too distracting. They began getting rowdy, so to calm them down I once again engaged them in conversation. Once they quieted down, I got the inevitable question:

"What else have you worked on?"

I told them that I had worked on *Hancock* and *The Taking of Pelham 123*." They were so excited to hear that I had seen Will Smith that they began shaking my hand. It was awkward. The crew had started staring at the small spectacle. I had the kids quietly and calmly asking me questions about movies. And then they started asking for autographs.

There I was, standing in front of the stars, my bosses, the producers, and my fellow PAs, signing autographs. Everyone is wondering what the hell is going on. But production is moving forward, the kids are not disturbing anyone, and we finish the scene. I wave goodbye to the kids, and a fellow PA approaches me.

"Were you really just signing autographs?"

At this moment the 2nd 2nd AD comes up wondering the same thing,

"What the hell was that? Why were you signing autographs on a lockup?"

I looked at him, gave him a knowing smile and said, "Kept 'em quiet, didn't it?" I got a fist bump for that one. Be creative, and remember: What we do may be a job to you, but it's an exciting mystery for the rest of the world.

INTERACTING WITH TALENT

Every so often on-set, and as a PA more often, you will find yourself interacting with talent. Talent can be anyone from the star whom you idolize to the background actor whom you despise. Handling talent is a true balancing act. Emotions can run high, schedules are run tight, and everything seems to be concrete, until it is changed. To begin this section let's discuss the way in which a PA may interact with talent.

THE MEET AND GREET

When talent arrives on-set they're going to walk by you. Don't be afraid. Make eye contact, if the vibe is right, offer a handshake and introduce yourself. Remember, no matter how big they look on screen, they're just people. Once the talent knows you, they may call on you to find out where they can relax. In this case show the talent to their chair or their mark by the camera. This is the most common way in which a PA will interact with talent.

CUEING TALENT

Every so often a PA will be called upon to cue an actor. Cueing means you tell the actor when to start or stop something in a scene. The PA will be hidden from camera, but within the actor's view. The AD will give the cue over the walkie to the PA, who will then pass the cue on to the actor, telling him or her to go. When working out a cue with an actor, ask them how they would prefer to be cued. Do they want something verbal or physical? Is a hand signal okay? Oh, here's a big no-no. Be careful what you say when you are cueing actors. They are wearing microphones that lead straight into the director, producer, and AD's headsets. Everyone is listening.

Besides cueing principal actors, a PA may be called upon to help set and cue the background actors. Cueing can be as simple as telling an actor when to cross the set or as complicated as timing out traffic lights so an actor can safely run through a jammed intersection. When dealing with background actors, the first thing to do is be nice. Smile, joke, and put them at ease so that they are more inclined to listen to you. It goes a long way. When you set background, be sure that they clearly understand their assigned walking path and their assigned action. I once shot an art auction at Sotheby's in New York. This is where a background actor bent all the way forward to smell some flowers on a table, where he was perfectly framed in the center of the picture between our heroes in the foreground. He didn't last much longer that day.

BE COURTEOUS AND RESPECTFUL — DON'T LOSE YOUR COOL

Try to relate to background actors. They are small fish in a big pond and everyone needs a friend at work. Be nice to these folks. In my experience, they respond better to jokes, sarcastic wit, and suggestion, than to orders and commands.

One of the most powerful tools you have when dealing with talent is the ability to be pleasant. Take every situation in stride and try not to let it overwhelm you. At the end of the day it's just a job and you should leave work at the door... or at least in the van ride home.

SECOND UNIT

In order to keep a film on schedule, second units are created to lighten the burden of a heavy shooting schedule. These units will shoot scenes that do not involve principal actors, or scenes where doubles may be used. An example of this would be driving shots. If the camera is filming a car as it speeds down the road, do we need to have the real actor drive it? The answer is no. The actor may take that day off or shoot a different scene with the main unit, and the production gets the driving shot in the can.

THE CREW

Second units are basically a reduced crew. They are a great way for a PA to get face time with important people. Usually a few PAs will be accompanied by one producer who may act as a "second unit director," one or two ADs, a grip, a three-man camera team, and an electrician. Everyone besides the camera crew usually splinters off from the main unit for the day. Because a camera team is so important to a production, a second camera team is hired for second units so that the director and his camera department can continue to work their magic.

SECOND UNIT VS. SPLINTERS

A splinter unit is a unit that breaks away from the main unit for a short period of time. For example, on a two-camera television show, the B-camera may move to an area away from the action of the current scene. There, they will shoot insert shots that will be needed later. After a few hours of inserts, the B-camera rejoins the main unit and continues shooting. This is called a splinter unit. If the unit starts the day separately from the main unit, and ends separately as well, it is known as a second unit.

PHOTO SHOOTS

Photo shoots are like the diamond in the rough for PAs. While most days you will work with moving images, photo shoots (still photography) only require a quick snap and thus less setup time.

Photo shoots are necessary to create the needed props and set dressing for a realistic film. The beauty of a photo shoot is that you don't need nearly as much prep time and the actual shooting is not based on the size of a scene. If you plan everything and multitask properly you will be able to blow through photo shoots with no problem. Here's what you need to know.

WHO'S INVOLVED?

A photo crew will usually consist of at least one grip for holding a bounce card and setting up stands, one electrician to rig the lights and direct them properly, one Prop representative, one stylist from Hair, one Makeup artist, and one Wardrobe representative. There will also be at least one member of production (usually a PA and a 2nd AD), a photographer, and talent. This is called a skeleton crew and is relatively typical of most photo shoots.

STAY ORGANIZED AND ON SCHEDULE

For PAs, this means a lot more responsibility. While you still look to the ADs for guidance, you are now more in control than you've ever been. You troubleshoot any problems that arise and if you can't shoot one shot, you should have the next one lined up and ready so you can go straight into it. Always have a backup plan. If you can't get the shot you need now, what else can you do to keep moving forward?

We have our schedule, our actors are all dressed, checked in, and through Hair and Makeup. Next we head over to location. Make sure that you have all of your elements (another word for crewmembers — each department can be considered an element) together. This means that your grip has his bounce board and white card and is ready to roll. Your electrician has the lights rigged and is set. The Prop representative has all the rings the actor will wear plus the frying pan that he is displaying for the photo and the Hair, Makeup, and Wardrobe reps are with you to do last touches before you shoot.

SHOOT AND GO HOME EARLY

Now that you've got all the elements in place and are on location, it's time to shoot your photos… then go home. It's always a pleasure to work photo shoots because it's like working on an independent film. Sometimes you just have to go guerrilla and it's a fun experience. As a PA it's a great multitasking experience because you are balancing and juggling the entire shoot while the 2nd AD is supervising and working on the main film unit.

MOVING VEHICLES

Ever wonder how the cameramen get those shots of people driving in cars without strapping themselves to the sides and praying? Well, here's your answer.

PROCESS TRAILER

There are multiple rigs used today. The most common is called a process trailer. The process trailer is a large bed attached to the back of a flatbed truck. The truck has a bench in the back as well as a rail to which a monitor can be attached. The trailer itself has a car on it. The car will never move, but the cameraman will strap himself to the trailer and film while the truck pulls it around, creating the illusion of driving. As long as the scenery keeps changing, who really notices?

When the trailer takes off, the necessary crew will trail behind them in a follow van. The follow van is used to carry crew, extra supplies, and to block traffic for the process trailer. Now, once the trailer and the vans take off, a PA must stay behind at the base to make sure that no one

A process trailer, used to create the illusion of driving when the script requires that actors are filmed inside a "moving" vehicle. © *Dan Brosnan 2009.*

parks in the trailer's spot and that all of the equipment stays safe while the procession makes its rounds. Once the trailer lands, your job becomes keeping the crew safe until everyone is out of the street.

CAMERA CAR

When the film audience does not need to hear what is going on inside a car, a camera car is used. It's a truck with a bench for crew, and trusses to hold monitors and equipment. The camera is fixed to the bed of the truck with the crew, while the picture car drives alongside separately. This allows a director to capture moving shots of vehicles from wider angles. I was working on the second unit of a movie *Get Him to the Gig* in New York when I got to spend a day getting driving shots on the 59th Street Bridge (connects Manhattan to Queens) with two police cars and a camera rig. It was amazing to see the action on the monitors while the car was driving alongside of us. The actors inside were having an expressive argument on the bridge that would be filmed later, but we got to capture the physical comedy. For more excitement though, I turn to the next rig.

The crew straps in to the railings and benches to stay safe... talk about the wind in your hair!

A camera car holds the camera and the crew for driving shots that involve the exterior of a moving car. © *Joshua A. Friedman 2009.*

PURSUIT CAR

The crane swivels 360 degrees to get really cool shots at a fast pace.

A pursuit car has a large crane on the top that holds a camera for complicated driving stunts. © *Joshua A. Friedman 2009.*

A new goodie that I just learned about is called a pursuit car. I learned about this rig while working on a sci-fi movie called *The Adjustment Bureau.* The pursuit car that we were using was a BMW with an armored body and a crane extension coming off the top. The long crane arm extended a good thirty feet away from the body of the car. It was incredibly cool to watch this car follow our hero's vehicle up and down 10th Avenue in Manhattan, while weaving in and out of traffic with its moving roof-mounted camera. When I watched the footage it looked like the camera was floating through the cars.

A Note about Moving Vehicles

Listen up when you are working with moving vehicles. Any time a trailer is about to move it will honk it's horn. Three beeps signal the crew to clear away, this baby's about to be on the move. The same is true when a vehicle stops. Once the trailer comes to a complete stop, the crew must wait for the honks to signal that it is safe to start dismounting.

DIFFERENT TYPES OF WORK DAYS

The life of a production assistant is completely unpredictable. An average workday can last anywhere from 12 to 20 hours or more. You will most likely see the sun both rise and set on a daily basis. Monday you will go to work at 4:00 a.m., and by Friday you're not coming in until 12:00 p.m. It's hard to make plans outside of work and it's hard to balance a sleep schedule. But it's very possible. Eventually your body will adjust and the schedule will become normal.

Film schedules will be different from television schedules. Film sets tend to work longer hours and odd work weeks. On a television show you will most likely work Monday through Friday. On a feature film you may work Sunday through Thursday. The schedule changes based on the needs of production.

PAs work on what we call a rolling schedule. This means that the start time of your workday is not set. We do not work from nine to five every day. Instead, the start of our day is determined by the end time of the previous day's work.

TURNAROUND

The time period beginning from the moment a crewmember is off the clock until their call time the following workday is known as turnaround. There are two turnaround rules that determine when actors and crewmembers may come back to work:

Rule No. 1: Cast Turnaround: If a castmember is working in the last scene of the current shoot day and the first scene of the following shoot day, production must allow the castmember twelve (12) hours of rest time off the clock.

Rule No. 2: Crew Turnaround: If cast turnaround is not an issue, crewmembers will be given ten (10) hours of rest time off the clock starting from the time their department wraps.

Sometimes the schedule does not allow for an actor to receive his full 12 hours of turnaround. In this situation, production has two options. They may choose to force an actor to come in early, or if applicable, they may invoke the 11-hour overnight turnaround rule.

If an actor is forced to come into work early it is known as "invading an actor's turnaround." Production will try their hardest not to force a call because it will come with a stiff monetary penalty. In some cases a forced call can be avoided:

Rule No. 3: An actor can be given an 11-hour turnaround three times in one work week on non-consecutive days.

The 11-hour rule can only be invoked with the approval of the actor and the UPM. It is most often used to keep a production on schedule when shooting time goes over.

If shooting time does go over, rather than invade an actor's turn-around, production may opt to change the next day's call time.

PUSHING AND PULLING THE CALL

At the end of your shooting day production will be faced with one of three options for starting work the next day. If today's shoot must run late, tomorrow's call time may be pushed. Pushing a call means making it later. For example, if the call time is 8:00 a.m. and call has been pushed one hour, then crew call becomes 9:00 a.m. The reverse is true for a pulled call. If production pulls the call, it means you will start the day earlier. This happens when production finishes before expected. The third option is to let the call stand. This means it will stay exactly as it is written on the call sheet.

In order to push or pull a call time, a PA will need either a red stamp which reads "ALL CALLS __ LATER" or a green stamp which reads "ALL CALLS __ EARLIER." These will be used to mark the call sheets with the correct call time before they are handed to the crew.

STAMPING THE CALL SHEETS

At some point, you will be told that call time has to be pushed and the call sheets need to be stamped. You will most likely receive this information ten minutes before the call sheets are needed on-set.

Here is a simple process for stamping that most ADs will find effective.

1. Lay out the call sheets in columns on a hard surface. Only leave the top part of the call sheet visible and use as many columns as you need.

2. Take a Sharpie (green for earlier, red for later) and mark a slash through the call time.

3. Use your "ALL CALLS__ EARLIER/LATER" stamps on the upper left corner of each call sheet.

4. When the AD tells you how far the call is pushed or pulled, write that number in the "__" portion of the stamp.

5. To the right of the printed call time, write down the adjusted call time in big clear handwriting.

Take these stamped call sheets to set and hope you've got them there before wrap!

Now that we know how much time a crewmember is given away from the workplace, let's discuss the types of days that you will experience on the job.

THE DAYLIGHT-DEPENDENT SHOOT

When a shoot is daylight-dependent, the schedule is limited by the amount of sunlight available during the day. These will tend to be shorter days because you are constrained by the availability of sunlight. A daylight-dependent shoot will start before the sun rises so that when dawn's light is strong enough, everything on-set is ready to go.

DAY SHOOT

The day shoot is the most common type of shoot that you will encounter. It is the closest thing to working normal business hours that you will experience in the industry. Day shoots start around 6:00 a.m. and end around 8:00 p.m. It is known as an average day.

SPLITS

Splits will find you arriving at work between 12:00 p.m. and 3:00 p.m. and going home between 3 a.m. and 5:00 a.m. These days are called splits because they split the shooting day into half daylight and half nighttime. Days like this can throw off your sleep schedule, so be prepared. If you go to bed too early the night before, you may not have energy to make it through the second half at nighttime. Plan accordingly.

NIGHT SHOOT

Night shoots take place when the sun has gone down. They are similar to day shoots and will usually be found on the schedule after a split. For this shoot, be prepared to stay up late. You will go into work between 5:00 p.m. and 7:00 p.m. and come home between 7:00 a.m. and 9:00 a.m.

OVERNIGHT SHOOT

When your call time is after 7:00 p.m. you will be shooting an overnight. Odds are you saw the sun set on your way to work and you will see it rise again before you go home. This job will end around 10:00 a.m. the following day. Overnight shoots may be used to shoot highly populated locations, such as Grand Central Station or a high school, at times when they will be empty. From a PA perspective, overnights can be daunting. Try not to book back-to-back jobs with these nights, as some of us do. Take care of yourself.

THE PAPERWORK

Prioritizing Distro

As a Paperwork PA on-set, I constantly receive distro from the office throughout the day. My responsibility is to deliver the packages to the crew in a timely fashion. My day is filled with constant activity. Running around, logging progress, and reporting back to the office keeps me pretty busy. In between these tasks I assist all of the other PAs on-set if or when they need an extra hand. Now, printing the call sheet is one of the most important aspects of a Paperwork PA's job. You must make copies, staple attachments, and have them on-set before the camera wraps. The call sheet is usually released no more than twenty to thirty minutes before wrap. Inevitably; a distro run will always come while you are in the middle of this process. What do you do?

I stop stapling and sort through the distro looking for key items. In this case a key item would be something for the director, producer, or ADs. Usually this information is time-sensitive. After the sorting I finish stapling my call sheets and head down to set, packages in hand. On-set I first pass the call sheets to the Key PA. Once he has those in hand, it's time to get back to the rest of your job. Deliver the priority distro and, if there is still time before wrap, you can pass out the remaining items. Remember, don't stress out. When you are in a crunch, there is always "first thing in the morning."

THE CALL SHEET

On the next page you will see an example of a call sheet (the names have been changed to protect the innocent). The call sheet is the one piece of paper that will answer 90% of your questions. Learn how to read it and find the information you need. Following the example, I will describe each section on the front of the call sheet and the information within.

SECTION 1
SECTION 2
SECTION 3
SECTION 4
SECTION 5
SECTION 6
SECTION 7

GETTING IT DONE

Director:	**Crew Call**	Date: Weekday, Day, Month, Year
Executive Producer:		Day ___ of ___
Producer:	**TIME**	Sunrise: ___ Sunset: ___
Writer:		
UPM:		Weather:
Co-Producer:	**Shoot Call**	
	Van Pick Ups	

SET/SCENE DESCRIPTION	SCENE #	CAST	D/N	PGS	LOCATION
INT HAMPTON'S APARTMENT *Hampton discusses his new job with Cowboy*	28	1,2,3,6	N2	1 1/8	**26-49 Central Park Ave. New York, NY**
COMPANY MOVE					
EXT HAMPTON'S BUILDING *Hampton pickpockets a Lawyer*	33	1,7	D4	3/8	**29-543 West 49th Street**
			Total:	1 4/8	

CAST

#	CAST	CHARACTER	STAT	PU/RPT	H/MU/W	REH	ON SET	NOTES
1	Wade Clark	HAMPTON	SW	P/U @	7:00 AM	7:30 AM	8:00 AM	Van #1 P/U @
2	Cassidy Bent	JORRY	W	P/U @				
3	Adam Rothstein	MR. DOUGLAS	WF	P/U @				
5	Jenn Melfried	ADRIENNE	H	HOLD	HOLD	HOLD	HOLD	
6	Joshua A. Friedman	COWBOY	W	P/U @				
7	Chelsea Roman	LAWYER	SWF	P/U @				

Sc.	BACKGROUND	P/U @	RPT	SPECIAL INSTRUCTIONS		
	S.I.'s:					
	#1,#2	N/A	7:00 AM	**Props:**	Sc 28	Coffee mugs, fresh coffee, bunt cake
	#3,#6 (pulled from count)	N/A	9:00 AM		Sc 33	Strollers, pocketwatch
28	0 bg			**Hair/MU:**	Sc 33	Hampton's Bloody Lip
33	10 Passerbys		8:00 AM	**Grips:**	Sc 28	Day for Night
	5 Business types (w/ suits)			**Add'l Labor:**	Sc 28	photographer, voice coach
	2 Park ladies with strollers					
	4 College teens (w/ backpacks)					
	ALL BG COME H/MU READY					
	Total SAG: 21 Total SI: 2					

BASECAMP	CREW PARKING/CATERING	HOSPITAL	BASECAMP

ADVANCE SCHEDULE					
SET/SCENE DESCRIPTION	SCENE #	CAST	D/N	PGS	LOCATION
PROD. DAY - DAY, DATE, MONTH, YEAR					
MORE SCENES	SCENE #	CAST	D/N	PAGES	LOCATION
			Total:		
PROD. DAY - DAY, DATE, MONTH, YEAR					
MORE SCENES	SCENE #	CAST	D/N	PAGES	LOCATION
			Total:		

Production Company	UPM:
Address	1st AD:
City, State, Zip	Key 2nd AD:
Phone # Fax # SET CELL PHONE #	2nd 2nd AD:

Courtesy of the author.

Project Title Crew Call: TIME Date: Date: Weekday, Day, Month, Year

PRODUCTION

1	Director	7:00 AM
1	Producer	O/C
1	Producer	
1	Producer	
1	Executive Producer	
1	UPM	
1	Co-Producer	

ASSISTANT DIRECTORS - Channels 1,2,3

1	1st AD	7:00 AM
1	Key 2nd AD	7:00 AM
1	2nd 2nd AD	7:00 AM
1	Key PA	7:00 AM
1	Set PA	7:00 AM
1	Set PA	7:00 AM
1	Set PA	7:00 AM
1	Set PA	7:00 AM

SCRIPT

1	Script Supervisor	7:00 AM

CAMERA - Channel 7

1	Dir. of Photography	7:00 AM
1	A Cam Operator	7:00 AM
1	A Cam 1st AC	7:00 AM
1	A Cam 2nd AC	7:00 AM
1	DIT Tech	7:00 AM
1	Camera PA	7:00 AM
	Still Photographer	-

ELECTRICIANS - Channel 6

1	Gaffer	7:00 AM
1	Best Boy Electric	7:00 AM
1	Genny Op	7:00 AM
1	Electrician	7:00 AM
1	Rigging Gaffer	7:00 AM

GRIPS - Channel 5

1	Key Grip	7:00 AM
1	BB Grip	7:00 AM
1	Dolly Grip	7:00 AM
1	Company Grip	7:00 AM
1	Company Grip	7:00 AM
1	Rigging Grip	7:00 AM

SOUND

1	Sound Mixer	7:00 AM
1	Boom Operator	7:00 AM
1	Sound Utility	

ART DEPARTMENT

1	Prod. Designer	O/C
1	Art Director	O/C
1	Art Dept Coord	O/C
1	Art PA	O/C

CONSTRUCTION

1	Construction Coordinator	O/C

SET DECORATION - Channel 1

1	Set Decorator	O/C
1	Lead Man	Per AM
1	Set Dec PA	Per AM
1	Set Dresser	Per AM
1	Set Dresser	Per AM
1	On Set Dresser	7:00 AM

SCENIC - Channel 4

1	Camera Scenic	7:00 AM

PROPS - Channel 4

1	Prop Master	7:00 AM
1	Asst Prop Master	7:00 AM
1	Prop	7:00 AM

WARDROBE

1	Costume Designer	O/C
1	Asst. Costume Designer	O/C
1	Wardrobe Supervisor	7:00 AM
1	Costumer	7:00 AM
1	Costumer	7:00 AM
1	Costume PA	7:00 AM

MAKE UP & HAIR

1	Dept Head Makeup	7:00 AM
1	Key Makeup Artist	7:00 AM
1	Dept Head Hair	7:00 AM
1	Key Hair Stylist	7:00 AM

LOCATIONS - Channel 1

1	2nd AD/Loc Mgr	O/C
1	Asst. Loc Manager	
1	Asst. Loc Manager	
1	Location Coordinator	
1	Unit PA	
1	Parking Coord.	O/C

ADDITIONAL CREW

1	Publicist	O/C
1	Clearances	O/C

SPECIAL EFFECTS

1	Special Effects	-

PRODUCTION OFFICE

1	Prod Coord	O/C
1	Asst. Prod. Coord.	O/C
1	Office P.A.	O/C
1	Office P.A.	O/C

POST-PRODUCTION / EDITING

1	Post Production Supervisor	O/C
1	Editor	O/C
1	Asst Editor	O/C
1	Music Supervisor	O/C

ACCOUNTING

1	Production Acct.	O/C
1	Payroll Accountant	O/C

CASTING

1	Casting Director	O/C
1	Casting Associate	O/C
1	Extras Casting	O/C
1	Extras Casting	O/C

CATERING/CRAFT SERVICE

1	Caterer		
1	Chef		
1	Chef		
	Crew Breakfast for :	Ready @	6:00 AM
	BG Breakfast for: 0	Ready @	-
	Crew Lunch for :	Ready @	12:30 PM
	BG Lunch for : 0	Ready @	-
1	Craft Service		
	Craft Service for:	Ready @	8:00 AM

TRANSPORTATION - Channel 16

1	Transportation Capt.	O/C
1	Transportation Co-Capt.	O/C
1	Van #1	
1	Van #2	
1	Van #3	
1	Set Dec Truck	
1	Electric Truck	
1	Grip Truck	
1	HMU Truck	
	Wardrobe Truck	
	Honeywagon	
	Camera Truck	

per

SPECIAL EQUIPMENT

TRANSPORTATION NOTES:

Courtesy of the author.

Section 1 — Production Info

- Production contact information
- Production company and show title
- Crew call (not to be confused with shooting call)
- The date and the day of the shoot (e.g., day 3 of 8)
- Weather report, sunrise and sunset times

Section 2 — Shooting Schedule

- Scene titles
  - Indicates if scene is interior (INT) or exterior (EXT)
  - Contains a brief scene description
- Scene numbers
- Castmembers in a scene
  - Indicated by numbers. Each number refers to a specific castmember.
- Which day or night the scene is within the context
- The page length of each scene
  - Pages are divided into 1/8-page increments. An 1/8 is about the width of a ruler (1 inch).
- The specific, mapquestable (I know it's not a real word) location (be sure to include a ZIP code) where the crew will be shooting

Section 3 — The Cast

- Numbers next to assigned actor names
  - Number 1 will always be the main star
  - Stuntperson numbers always begin in the 100s
- Cast (actor) name
  - Character name
- Status
  - SW — Start Work
  - W — Working
  - WF — Work Finish
  - W/D — Work Drop (off-days falling between shooting days for which a principal actor will not be paid)
  - SWF — Start Work Finish (the player is hired for one day)
  - H — Hold (the actor is not called in that day)
  - PH — The actor is called in for a photo

— W/N — Will Notify (the actor will be called later that day to come in at a certain time)
- Report time (arrival time)
- Rehearsal time
- Hair and Makeup time
- Time due on-set
- The time that the actor will be picked up and their transportation
  — Van pickup or car pickup

Section 4 — Background

- Stand-ins for each character number and their report times
- Breakdown of scenes
  — Number of background actors per scene
  — Types of background in each scene
    ▪ Ex: uniformed officers, CSU techs, passersby
  — Total number of stand-ins, SAG actors, and non-SAG actors

Section 5 — Special Instructions

- Departmental needs
  — Props — listed by the scene they will be used in
  — Vehicles — any used in the film
  — Costumes — special wardrobe notes
  — Hair/Makeup — any scars, tattoos, etc., needed
  — Special FX — any special effects required
  — Additional labor — set medics, safety divers for underwater or waterside shoots, etc.

Section 6 — Locations

- Location of base camp, working trucks, holding/catering, etc.
- Nearest hospital with phone number and address

Section 7 — Advance Schedule

- A copy of Section 2 that shows the schedule for the following day

On the back of the call sheet you will find a long list. This list has the name of every crewmember working that particular day. It also has the in-time for those crewmembers. At the bottom of the back of the call sheet, there is a transportation section that will tell you the time and location of vans to set in the morning. GOOD LUCK!

THE PRODUCTION REPORT (PR)

On the following page you will see an example of a production report. Similar to a call sheet in that it contains a wealth of information, the production report (PR) summarizes the events of the entire shooting day. It is invaluable for producers, ADs, and the Accounting/Payroll Department. Make sure that you know and understand how to read one of these because they teach you more about the business side of the industry. After the example I will explain the PR sections in more detail.

MOVIE TITLE

DAILY PRODUCTION REPORT

DAY of the Week, Month Day, Year

Shoot Day: 23 of 45

Production Company
Address

Phone number
Fax number

Director:
Producer:
Producer:
Producer/UPM:
Writer:
AUPM:
1st AD: , 2nd AD:

CREW CALL	8:00 AM
FIRST SHOT	First time camera rolls
1ST MEAL OUT	Meal Break time
1ST MEAL IN	Meal Back in time
1ST SHOT	1st Shot after lunch
2ND MEAL OUT	
2ND MEAL IN	
1ST SHOT 2ND MEAL	
CAMERA WRAP	8:00 PM
LAST MAN OUT	Last worker off the clock

START DAY:	Start Date
EST FINISH:	Completion Date
SUNRISE/SET:	sunrise and sunset
HIGH/LOW:	Temperature Highs and lows
WEATHER:	Daily weather

		HOLIDAY	IDLE	TEST	WORK	TOTAL	
# DAYS SCHED.	*		0	3	45	48	+/-
# DAYS ACTUAL	*		0	3	26	26	0

SC	I/E	SET/DESCRIPTION	D/N	CAST	PGS	LOCATION
B192	I/E	PSYCH HOSPITAL - PARKING LOT - MEREDITH'S CAR	D46	2,3,5	4/8	Denver VA Hospital
		Meredith gets into her car with the kids				1125 Grand Concourse
A192	E	PSYCH HOSPITAL	D46	3	1/8	San Friedo, PA 20342
		Meredith reacts to the news				
194	E	PSYCH HOSPITAL	D47	1,2,3,5	2/8	
		Bob takes his medication				
A170	E	PSYCH HOSPITAL	D45	1,2,5	3/8	
		Meredith talks with the Doctor				
168	I	PSYCH HOSPITAL - GROUP THERAPY	D43	1,10	2/8	
		Sam gets Bob to open up				
167	E	PSYCH HOSPITAL - GROUNDS	D41	1	2/8	
		Bob tries to escape				
				TOTAL PAGES	1 6/8	

	PAGES	SCENES	MINUTES	SETUPS	ADD/DEL	SCENES SCHEDULED TODAY	ROLLS	CAM A	CAM B	VIDEO	SOUND	WLD TRX
TOTAL	114 2/8	190				B192,A192,194,A170,168,167	PREV	212	0	0	26	15
PREV	63 2/8	83	1:07:07	320	2	SCENES COMPLETED TODAY	TODAY	5	0	0	1	1
TODAY	1 2/8	5	0:02:42	14	0	A192,B192,(A170),194,167,168	TO DATE	217	0	0	27	16
TO DATE	64 4/8	88	1:09:49	334	2	SCENES SHOT NOT SHOT	ROLL/ TRACK #S	Rolls A166- A170			27	
REMAIN	49 6/8	102				N/A			-	-		1016

Notes: 1. Scene A170 unscripted. Has no official Page count and is not included in the scene count. No deductions apart from time and setups

SCENES SCHEDULED TODAY

SCENES SHOT NOT SCHEDULED TODAY

N/A

* 35MM FILM INVENTORY - BY STOCK # *

6219 (500T)	LOADED	PRINT	NO PRINT	WASTE	SHOT/USED	SHORT ENDS		RAW STOCK	LOADED	RECEIVED	STOCK # SUMMARY	
PREV	123040	63380	29200	9330	101910	PREV S.E.	7690	PREV	109600	153000	TOTAL RAW	43400
TODAY	900	330	140	0	470	MADE TODAY	430	TODAY	0	0	TOTAL S.E.	7220
TO DATE	123940	63710	29340	9330	102380	USED TODAY	900	TO DATE	109600	153000	TOTAL ON HAND	50620
						S.E. ON HAND	7220	RAW ON HAND	43400			

* 35MM FILM INVENTORY - ALL STOCKS *

TOTAL STOCKS	LOADED	PRINT	NO PRINT	WASTE	SHOT/USED	SHORT ENDS		RAW STOCK	LOADED	RECEIVED	TOTAL STOCK AVERAGES	
PREV	123040	63380	29200	9330	101910	PREV S.E.	7690	PREV	109600	153000	PREV AVERAGE	6153.64
TODAY	900	330	140	0	470	MADE TODAY	430	TODAY	0	0	SHOT TODAY	470
TO DATE	123940	63710	29340	9330	102380	USED TODAY	900	TO DATE	109600	153000	DAILY AVERAGE	4451.30
TOTAL FOOTAGE ON HAND				7220		S.E. ON HAND	7220	RAW ON HAND	43400			

* 16MM FILM INVENTORY - BY STOCK # *

7219	LOADED	PRINT	NO PRINT	WASTE	SHOT/USED	SHORT ENDS		RAW STOCK	LOADED	RECEIVED	STOCK # SUMMARY	
PREV	1550	460	210	280	950	PREV S.E.	250	PREV	1200	1600	TOTAL RAW	400
TODAY	0	0	0	0	0	MADE TODAY	0	TODAY	0	0	TOTAL S.E.	250
TO DATE	1550	460	210	280	950	USED TODAY	0	TO DATE	1200	1600	TOTAL ON HAND	650
						S.E. ON HAND	250	RAW ON HAND	400			

#	CAST	CHARACTER	STATUS	REPORT H&MU	REPORT TO SET	DISMISS SET	DISMISS H&MU	N D R	1st MEAL OUT	1st MEAL IN	2nd MEAL OUT	2nd MEAL IN	LEAVE S'TG/ HOME	ARRIVE S'TG/ LOC	LEAVE S'TG/ LOC	ARRIVE HOME
1	ADAM WEINSTEIN	BOB	W	8:30 AM	10:00 AM	4:30 PM	4:45 PM		12:00 PM	1:00 PM	-	-	8:00 AM	8:30 AM	4:45 PM	5:15 PM
2	MARJ N.M YANG	MEREDITH	W	6:45 AM	8:15 AM	4:30 PM	4:45 PM		12:00 PM	1:00 PM	-	-	6:15 AM	6:45 AM	4:45 PM	5:15 PM
3	JOSHUA ADAMS	DAVID	W	7:30 AM	8:30 AM	1:00 PM	1:15 PM		12:00 PM	1:00 PM	-	-	6:45 AM	7:30 AM	1:15 PM	2:00 PM
4	JENNIFER MELISSA	NORAH	H	-	-	-	-		-	-	-	-	-	-	-	-
5m	MARK ROMO	THE DOCTOR	W	7:30 AM	8:30 AM	1:00 PM	1:15 PM		12:00 PM	1:00 PM	-	-	6:45 AM	7:30 AM	2:15 PM	3:00 PM
10	DOUGLAS ANDREW	SAM	WF	1:00 PM	3:30 PM	4:30 PM	4:45 PM		-	-	-	-	-	1:00 PM	4:45 PM	-

#	TYPE	RATE	IN	OUT	N D B	1st MEAL IN	1st MEAL OUT	2nd MEAL IN	2nd MEAL OUT	T.H.	O.T.	ADJ/FEES	KEY	BG TOTALS	
1	SI/SA	159	7:00 AM	3:00 PM	-	1:45 PM	2:15 PM	-	-	8.0	0.0	2L	A=AUTO B=BUMP BY=BICYCLE	SI'S	
1	SI	149	7:00 AM	5:00 PM	-	1:00 PM	2:00 PM	-	-	9.0	1.0		#C=# CHANGE(S) D=DOG	PREV	58
1	SI	149	9:00 AM	5:00 PM	-	1:45 PM	2:15 PM	-	-	8.0	0.0		#F=# FORMAL C(S) H=HAZARD	TODAY	3
3	SAG	134	7:00 AM	4:00 PM	-	1:00 PM	2:00 PM	-	-	8.0	0.0	Auto	M=MILEAGE MU=MAKE UP NS=NON-SAG	TO DATE	61
3	SAG	134	7:00 AM	4:30 PM	-	1:00 PM	2:00 PM	-	-	8.5	0.5		#P=# PROP(S) PD=PHOTO	SAG BG	
14	SAG	134	10:00 AM	4:30 PM	-	2:00 PM	3:00 PM	-	-	8.0	0.0		DOUBLE S=SMOKE	PREV	516
													SA=SPECIAL ABILITY SB=SAG BG	TODAY	20
													SI=STAND IN SW=SAG WAIVER	TO DATE	536
													T=TRANSPO TX=TAXI	NON-SAG BG	
													U=UNIFORM W=WET	PREV	32
													WA=WALKAWAY WG=WIG	TODAY	0
														TO DATE	32
														TOTAL BG TODAY	23
														TOTAL BG	629

Prod/UPM -   AUPM -   1st AD -

MY MOVIE

DAY of the Week, Month Day, Year   Shoot Day: 23 of 45

#	DEPT/ POSITION	NAME	IN	OUT	MP
	PRODUCTION				
1	Director		8:00 AM	8:00 PM	
1	Executive Producer		O/C		
1	Producer		O/C		
1	Producer		O/C		
1	Producer/UPM		O/C		
1	AUPM		O/C		
	ASST DIRECTORS				
1	1st AD		8:00 AM	8:00 PM	
1	2nd AD		6:12 AM	9:00 PM	
1	2nd 2nd AD		7:42 AM	9:00 PM	
1	Key Set PA		6:12 AM	9:00 PM	
1	Set PA		6:12 AM	9:00 PM	
1	Set PA		6:12 AM	9:00 PM	
1	Set PA		6:12 AM	9:00 PM	
1	Set PA		6:12 AM	9:00 PM	
1	Addl PA		6:12 AM	9:00 PM	
1	Addl PA		6:12 AM	9:00 PM	
1	Addl PA		6:12 AM	9:00 PM	
	SCRIPT				
1	Script Supervisor		8:00 AM	5:30 PM	2L
	CAMERA				
1	DP		8:00 AM	8:00 PM	
1	"A" Camera Op		8:00 AM	5:30 PM	2L
1	"A" Camera 1st AC		8:00 AM	5:30 PM	2L
1	"A" Camera 2nd AC		8:00 AM	5:30 PM	2L
	Loader		8:00 AM	5:30 PM	
1	Camera PA		8:00 AM	5:30 PM	
1	Stills Photographer		8:00 AM	5:00 PM	
	ELECTRICAL				
1	Gaffer		8:00 AM	6:18 PM	2L
1	Best Boy Electric		8:00 AM	6:18 PM	2L
1	Genny Op		8:00 AM	6:18 PM	2L
1	Electrician		8:00 AM	6:18 PM	2L
1	Electrician		8:00 AM	6:18 PM	2L
1	Electrician		8:00 AM	6:18 PM	2L
1	Add'l Genny Op		8:00 AM	6:18 PM	2L
1	Add'l Electrician		8:00 AM	6:18 PM	2L
1	Add'l Electrician		8:00 AM	6:18 PM	2L
1	Rigging Gaffer		8:00 AM	6:30 PM	
1	Rigging Gaffer		7:00 AM	5:30 PM	
	GRIP				
1	Key Grip		8:00 AM	7:00 PM	2L
1	Best Boy Grip		8:00 AM	7:00 PM	2L
1	Dolly Grip		8:00 AM	7:00 PM	2L
1	Grip		8:00 AM	7:00 PM	2L
1	Grip		8:00 AM	7:00 PM	2L
1	Grip		8:00 AM	7:00 PM	2L
1	Crane Dolly Grip		8:00 AM	7:00 PM	2L
1	Addl Grip		8:00 AM	7:00 PM	2L
1	Addl Grip		8:00 AM	7:00 PM	2L
1	Key Rigging Grip		6:00 AM	6:30 PM	
1	Rigging Best Boy		6:00 AM	6:30 PM	
	SOUND				
1	Sound Mixer		8:00 AM	5:30 PM	2L
1	Utility Sound		8:00 AM	5:30 PM	2L
1	Boom Operator		8:00 AM	5:30 PM	2L
	VIDEO				
1	Video Assist		8:00 AM	5:06 PM	2L
	PUBLICITY				
1	Unit Publicist		O/C		

#	DEPT/ POSITION	NAME	IN	OUT	MP
	MAKE UP				
1	Key Make-Up Artist		7:30 AM	5:12 PM	3L
1	Make-up Artist		8:00 AM	5:12 PM	2L
1	Addl Makeup Artist		8:00 AM	5:12 PM	
	HAIR				
1	Key Hair Stylist		7:30 AM	5:12 PM	3L
1	Hair Stylist		8:00 AM	5:12 PM	2L
1	Addl Hair Stylist		8:00 AM	5:12 PM	
	COSTUMES				
1	Costume Designer		O/C		
1	Asst. Costume Designer		O/C		
1	Wardrobe Supervisor		6:30 AM	5:12 PM	3L
1	Key Costumer		6:18 AM	4:48 PM	3L
1	Costumer		8:00 AM	5:12 PM	2L
1	Addl Costumer		8:00 AM	5:12 PM	1L
1	Costume Coordinator		Per SL		
1	Wardrobe PA		Per SL		
	FX				
1	SPFX Manufacturer		7:30 AM	5:30 PM	
1	VSFX		8:00 AM	5:00 PM	
1	VSFX		8:00 AM	5:00 PM	
	LOCATIONS				
1	Location Manager		O/C		
1	Asst Loc Manager		Per RS		
1	Location Assistant		Per RS		
	Location Assistant		Per RS		
1	Locatoin Coordinator		Per RS		
1	Unit PA		Per RS		
1	Location PA		Per RS		
	ART DEPT.				
1	Prod. Designer		O/C		
1	Art Director		Per MF		
1	Art Director		Per MF		
1	Graphics		Per MF		
1	Art Dept. Coordinator		Per MF		
1	Art Researcher		Per MF		
1	Art PA		Per MF		
1	Art PA		Per MF		
	PROPERTY				
1	Property Master		8:00 AM	5:30 PM	2L
1	Asst Prop Master		8:00 AM	5:30 PM	2L
1	3rd Prop		8:00 AM	5:30 PM	2L
	SET DECORATION				
1	Set Decorator		O/C		
1	Asst. Set Dec		Per RMD		
1	Leadman		Per RMD		
1	On-Set Dresser		8:00 AM	5:30 PM	2L
	GREENS				
1	Greensman		Per RMD		
1	Greensman		7:00 AM	6:00 PM	2L
	SCENIC				
1	Charge Scenic		O/C		
1	Scenic Foreman		O/C		
1	Standby Scenic		8:00 AM	5:06 PM	2L
	CONSTRUCTION				
1	Construction Coord.		O/C		
1	Construction Co-Coord.		O/C		
	SPECIAL EQUIPMENT				
	VFX Witness Camera, Ritter Fan, Phoenix Crane				
	VEHICLES				
	Meredith's Car				

#	DEPT/ POSITION	NAME	IN	OUT	
	PRODUCTION OFFICE				
1	Production Coord		O/C		
1	Asst Prod Office Coord		Per DW		
1	Prod Secretary		Per DW		
1	Office PA		Per DW		
1	Office PA		Per DW		
1	Office PA		Per DW		
	POST PRODUCTION				
1	Editor		O/C		
1	Asst Editor		O/C		
	CASTING				
1	Casting Director		O/C		
1	Casting Associate		O/C		
1	Casting Assistant		O/C		
	ACCOUNTING				
1	Prod. Accountant		O/C		
1	1st Asst. Accountant		O/C		
1	2nd Asst. Accountant		O/C		
1	Payroll Accountant		O/C		
1	Accounting Clerk		O/C		
	CATERING				
1	Chef		PER AT		
1	1st Asst Chef		PER AT		
1	2nd Asst Chef		PER AT		
1	3rd Asst Chef		PER AT		
				ORDERED	ACTUAL
	Crew B'Fast	Ready @	7:00 AM	100	89
	Extras B'Fast	Ready @	7:00 AM	0	0
	Crew Lunch	Ready @	1:00 PM	80	90
	Extras Lunch	Ready @		0	0
	CRAFT SERVICE				
1	Key Craft Service		8:00 AM	6:00 PM	
1	Key Craft Service		8:00 AM	6:00 PM	
	Craft Service	Ready @	8:30 AM		
	BG Craft Service	Ready @	8:30 AM		
	TRANSPORTATION				
1	Transpo Captain		O/C		
1	Co-Captain		Per JB	Per JB	
1	Camera Truck		Per JB	Per JB	
1	Electric Trailer		Per JB	Per JB	
1	Wardrobe Trailer		Per JB	Per JB	
1	Makeup Trailer		Per JB	Per JB	
1	Construction Truck		Per JB	Per JB	
1	Greens Truck		Per JB	Per JB	
1	Set Dress Truck		Per JB	Per JB	
1	Set Dress Helper		Per JB	Per JB	
1	Set Dec Driver		Per JB	Per JB	
1	Star Car		Per JB	Per JB	
1	Director Car		Per JB	Per JB	
1	15-Pass Van #1		Per JB	Per JB	
1	15-Pass Van #2		Per JB	Per JB	
1	15-Pass Van #3		Per JB	Per JB	
1	15-Pass Van #4		Per JB	Per JB	
1	Grip Trailer		Per JB	Per JB	
1	Electric Rigging Truck		Per JB	Per JB	
1	Grip Rigging Truck		Per JB	Per JB	
	ADD'L VEHICLES				
	ADD'L LABOR				
1	Rigging Grip		6:00 AM	6:30 PM	
1	Rigging Grip		6:00 AM	6:30 PM	
1	Rigging Grip		6:00 AM	6:30 PM	
1	Prosthetic Fabricator		8:00 AM	5:00 PM	
1	Rigging Electric Best Boy		7:00 AM	5:30 PM	
1	Rigging Electric		8:00 AM	6:30 PM	
1	Rigging Electric Best Boy		8:00 AM	6:30 PM	
1	Rigging Electric		8:00 AM	6:30 PM	

PRODUCTION NOTES

1 A safety meeting was held at call.
2
3
4
5
6
7
8
9
10 D. Dreyer's outtime reflects her wrapout from home. She does not incur any penalties.

Section 1 — Production Info, Time and Date Tracking
- Production company contact info
- Name of Writer/Director/Producers/UPM
- Picture title, day of shooting, date
- Local weather and sunrise/set times
- Time tracking for the day
  - Crew Call
  - First Shot — The time the cameras first roll
  - Lunch Times
  - First Shot After Lunch — The time the cameras first roll after lunch
  - Camera Wrap
  - Last Man

Section 2 — Scheduling Info
- Scene numbers, scene locations and descriptions, scene time within the script, cast in each scene, and page counts
- The physical location at which you are shooting

Section 3 — Script Notes and Roll Tracking
- Script Info
  - Tracks total script information for project
  - Pages shot and pages remaining
  - Scenes shot and remaining
  - Minutes shot
  - Setups shot
  - Notes from the Script Supervisor
  - Scenes added or deleted
  - Scenes that were scheduled to be shot
  - Scenes that were completed
  - Scenes scheduled, but not shot
  - Scenes shot, but not scheduled
- Roll Tracking
  - Number of camera rolls used and their roll numbers
  - Number of sound rolls used
  - Number of wild tracks (sound without a corresponding film image) recorded that day and their titles

Section 4 — Film Inventories
- Inventories are broken up into types of stock. Within each stock section you will find
  - 3 rows with previous, today, and to-date totals
  - Loaded Column — This is all film loaded into the camera including short ends
  - Print Column — All film that will be printed at the lab
  - No Print Column — Film that was shot/used, but should not be printed because it is no good
  - Waste Column — Leftover film that is too short to be used for a take
  - Shot/Used Column — Total film exposed for the day. This is the total loaded minus the remaining short ends.
  - **Short End Section**
    - Short Ends made this day — Any leftover film long enough to be reused for inserts or shorter takes
    - Short Ends used this day — Any short ends loaded into the camera and shot
    - Short Ends on hand — a calculation that takes the previous short ends, adds the short ends made today, and subtracts the short ends used today
  - **Raw Stock Section**
    - Raw stock loaded means full canisters of film that were used. This does not include short ends used.
    - Film received — All film received by the Camera Department
    - Raw film on hand — calculations in which you take the total film received and subtract the film that's been loaded. The remainder is the raw film on hand.
  - **Stock Summary**
    - Total raw stock
    - Total short ends
    - Combine those two numbers for the total film on hand count.

Section 5 — Exhibit G
- (Covered under the 1st Team PA Section)

Section 6 — Background Breakdown

- (Covered under the Background PA section)

Section 7 — The Back

- Project title, date, shooting day
- Crewmember positions organized by department
- Crewmember names
- Crewmember in-times
- Crewmember out-times
- Meal Penalties incurred by crewmembers
- Special Equipment used (may be on the front)
- Vehicles used (may be on the front)
- Notes about events that happened during the shooting day

Notes to Filling Out the PR

- Copy the call sheet section into the top. List all scenes, even if they are not shot.
- Copy script note information
  - Make sure to double-check the math on times and page counts
- Copy the camera reports
  - Again double-check the math, and continue adding to Year-To-Date
- Copy the Exhibit G
- Copy the background breakdown
- Copy over the call times (from the call sheet)
- Copy the Out-Times (what time each crew stopped working)
- Notes Section — Write them in this order (or per production's request)
  1. List lunch break first
  2. List any penalties the cast or crew incurred and the reason
  3. List any special lunch breaks such as Hair, Makeup, or Wardrobe
  4. List any accidents, incidents, or delays

SCHEDULES

From the time that a script is finalized, the UPM or the ADs start working on the schedule. The first thing they will do is break the script down scene by scene. Each scene is listed on a strip of paper with the following information:

- Scene Number
- INT or EXT
- Location of scene (in the script) and a brief description
- Time of day in the script
- Which day or night it is in the script
- Page count for the scene
- The characters in the scene (labeled using numbers that correspond to the call sheet)
- Actual shooting location

These strips with scene-by-scene information are then arranged and rearranged to form the production schedule.

SHOOTING SCHEDULE

The shooting schedule includes every piece of information that will be needed throughout production. It contains information about every scene that involves props, set dressing, special effects (F/X), etc. It also lists information about characters and background as well as the scene information itself. Scenes are organized according to the shooting order for easy reference when preparing the call sheet.

ONE-LINER

The one-liner is an abridged version of the shooting schedule. The shooting schedule offers all of the information about each scene; the one-liner is simply the strips of paper described earlier. As the title implies, every scene in the schedule occupies one line. The scenes are listed in the order in which they will be shot. All company moves (the production moves from one location to another) are noted on the one-liner as well as the end of each shooting day.

DAY-OUT-OF-DAYS (DOOD)

The day-out-of-days is a graph that contains information about when actors or equipment will be needed on-set. The cast day-out-of-days is laid out with the characters' names on the left side of the grid, and potential work dates spread across the top. Each of the corresponding boxes will be labeled with the actors' work status.

An equipment day-out-of-days is the same as the cast's except it replaces the character names with the equipment that will be rented. This form is very handy when tracking which vehicles will be used on-set during a production or telling actors what their schedules will be.

TIME CARDS

We don't work for free. In order to get paid you must fill out a time card. Every PA has to fill them out at some point and every PA fills them out wrong at least once. As a Paperwork PA, I do all of the time cards for my department. For the PAs, this is a simple task; for ADs, the rules get a bit more complicated. On the next page you'll find a sample of a time card.

For the staff PAs on-set, I keep all of their time cards in a folder at my desk. This allows me to update their hours on a daily basis. The early prep work can save a lot of time on Friday night when all of the time cards need to be turned in.

For additional PAs on-set, I ask them to hold on to their time cards if they know they're working again in the same week (sometimes additional PAs will be booked for multiple work days). If they are not coming back, I have them fill out their times and I add the card to my folder. The reason I let the additional PAs fill out their own time cards is simple. It can be overwhelming. I fill out eight to ten time cards for my department every week, and that takes enough time. I don't need the added chore of filling out the additional PAs' time cards as well. It sounds mean, but you have to draw the line so that you do not overwork yourself. Besides, it gives them the opportunity to learn how to fill out a time card right!

(SAMPLE TIME CARD)

WORK				MEAL 1		MEAL 2					1X	1.5X	2X	MEAL PENALTY
CITY	STATE	DATE	DAY	CALL	OUT	IN	OUT	IN	WRAP	TOTAL HOURS				
			1											
			2											
			3											
			4											
			5											
			6											
			7											

TOTAL HOURS

PICTURE TITLE		PROD. #	GUAR. HOURS	RATE	WEEK-ENDING
EMPLOYEE NAME		SOCIAL SECURITY #	JOB CLASSIFICATION		ACCOUNT #
LOAN OUT COMPANY		FEDERAL ID #	LOCATION	FOREIGN	

COMMENTS:

EMPLOYEE SIGNATURE   X_____

AUTHORIZED BY   X_____

THE TIME-TRACKING SECTION

Filling out the time-tracking section of the card is simple. "Day 1" is the first day of the workweek. If the week-ending day on a job is Saturday, then Sunday is "Day 1." If your first shooting day of the week is Monday, you will start your time card on the "Day 2" line. Your Paperwork PA can tell you which days of the week correlate to the "Day 1, Day 2, ..." system. From left to right on your time-tracking grid, you will need to fill in the following information. (Several of the boxes can be skipped, or require information you wouldn't know; again, turn to your helpful Paperwork PA.) Remember that, depending on the company you work for, the time card can appear in different formats, but this sample layout gives you a good idea of what information you will enter.

1. City in which you are working
2. State in which you are working
3. The date (month/day is fine)
4. Your call time (when you start working)
5. Your meal break(s) start time — "Out"
6. Your meal break(s) end time — "In"
7. Your wrap time (when you finish working)
8. Your signature (bottom of the time card)

Your call time can be found on the back of the call sheet. Again, ask the Paperwork PA for the meal times. They are usually nominal, as meal breaks should not be taken out of PA hours. The Paperwork PA will also be able to give you your wrap time once all of the other crewmembers have gone home for the day.

THE IDENTIFICATION SECTION (IDS)

Beneath the time-tracking section of the time card, you will see a group of labeled boxes spanning the width of the page. This part is the identification section (IDS). The IDS contains all of the information that the payroll company will need to recognize you as an employee. Here are the parts that you need to fill out from left to right.

1. The picture title
2. The week-ending

3. Your name
4. Your Social Security Number (or the last four digits)
5. Job classification

Boxes not mentioned will require the help of your Paperwork PA the first time you fill out a time card.

The name of the project can be found on the call sheet. The week-ending day is set by accounting and changes from job to job. Ask the Paperwork PA about the week-ending day. Be sure to designate whether you have a staff position or an additional position in the job classification box. The pay rates between the two differ on some jobs.

I know this is an obvious one, but from experience, please… *do not forget to sign your time card!* It happens way too often, and some ADs will not approve a time card without a signature. When this happens… someone's not getting paid.

ASSISTANT DIRECTOR TIME CARDS

I said that assistant director time cards are more complicated than PA time cards. They are, but only in some aspects. The time part of an AD time card starts the same with the location and dates, but differs in that you will not need to put lunch times into their time cards. Instead you will either leave these two boxes blank or write over both of them the words "Meal Money." With this we come to one of the most important rules of AD time cards:

ADs get meal money ($28.00) if they are on the clock on or before 9:00 a.m. *and* off the clock on or after 7:30 p.m.

ADs will get meal money if and only if both criteria are met. As a PA you will have to check these times. If the AD does receive meal money you will write "Meal Money" over the lunch times. At the end of the workweek you'll count up the number of meal monies the AD has earned and write and circle that number in the box at the bottom of the time card labeled "Meal Money." Just because we like to backup our backups, in the comments section write, "Meal Money received on the following dates…."

Since you're already calculating times with the meal money, you might as well go the extra step and calculate the total number of hours worked by the ADs. This information leads us to some more time card rules. Here are the main 1st AD rules:

> If a 1st AD works more than fourteen (14) hours in a day, then he gets an "extended day," or 1.5 times his daily rate.
>
> If a 1st AD works more than sixteen (16) hours in a day, then he gets a "double day," or two times his daily rate.

To indicate these details on an AD's time card, we will re-examine our time-tracking section. To the right of the time grid you will see another set of boxes. Above these boxes you will notice three numbers: 1X, 1.5X, and 2X. These stand for straight time or standard rate (1X), time-and-a-half pay (1.5X), and double-time pay or twice the hourly rate (2X), respectively. Mark and circle an "X" in the box that corresponds to the hours that the AD worked. For instance, if an AD works 14.5 hours, you will circle an "X" under the 1.5X column. Once this is noted on the grid, you should again add a note to the comments section. This note should read, "Extended day on the following dates...." This information will help you complete the 1st AD's time card. Now we will move on to the 2nd AD.

The 2nd (or 2nd 2nd) AD's time card is similar to that of the 1st AD, with two differences. The 2nd AD does not get more money after working 14 hours. He may be entitled to a $50 DGA wrap allowance (a bonus, called a *bump*) some nights. The rules for a 2nd AD are as follows:

> If a 2nd AD (or 2nd 2nd) works more than sixteen (16) hours in one day, he will get an extended day.
>
> If there is only one 2nd AD working, he will get an extended day after fourteen (14) hours.

The rules for a 2nd AD differ because the 2nd AD will usually work one to three hours more than the 1st AD (at least on-set). To compensate for this, 2nd ADs are entitled to a DGA wrap allowance.

> The 2nd AD who stays the latest (to ensure that all crew wrap out properly) receives a $50 DGA wrap allowance on nights before the company moves to a new location.

If an AD is entitled to the wrap "bump," that must be indicated on the time card. To do this, create a special symbol such as a star or a box. Mark this symbol to the left of the day that the bump is earned. In the comments section add a note that reads, "* = $50 DGA Wrap Allowance on the following dates...." Once this is done you have completed your first set of time cards. Congratulations, now get them approved!

PETTY CASH

"Petty cash is a privilege, not a right." So says the Accounting Department. Petty cash (PC) is loose cash that can be used for any number of miscellaneous necessities or last-minute emergencies. There are two PAs on-set who will have petty cash. The 1st Team PA will have PC in case an actor needs anything. The Paperwork PA will have PC to use in case anyone else needs something.

PETTY CASH REQUEST

In order to get you started, we have to do a little bit of paperwork. You will first have to fill out two forms. The first is a W-9 form for tax purposes. The second form is a petty cash request form. You will only have to submit these forms once at the beginning of the job. The UPM will approve an amount ranging from $300 to $500. This money is called your petty cash "float." Once you receive your float, you will not need to request any more cash from production. From this point forward all money that you receive can be considered a reimbursement of your float.

Pop Quiz: You're on-set with a $300 float when ten PAs bring you three receipts each. What do you do? Just buy their receipts from them. Tally up the amounts and give away the cash. When your float is low or empty, it's time for the fun part. For this part we will need some supplies: It's a mix between a filing system and an arts and crafts project.

TAPING THE RECEIPTS

This project requires two or three white pieces of scrap paper, Scotch tape, and a pen. Before we use these supplies, let us first get organized.

Every receipt that you collect should have identifying information on it. Who was the receipt for? If it's a cab ride, where was it from or to? To organize your receipts, group them in chronological order from oldest to most recent. Once you have grouped your receipts, tape each one to the white sheets of paper, individually and still in chronological order. Something to be aware of at this point is that a PC envelope only has twenty-four lines on it. If you have more than 24 receipts, it's going to take a second envelope. Plan accordingly. Once all of your receipts have been taped down, write and circle a number in the corner of each one ranging from one to twenty-four. These will correspond to the numbers on the PC envelope.

THE PC ENVELOPE

Now that all of your receipts are prepped, it's time to fill out the information listed on the PC envelope. The top part is an identification section. The only information you will need is the name of the project, your name, the date, and your position on the crew. Each line of the PC envelope consists of a few boxes. For our purposes we will only use four.

In the left-most box you will write the date. The box next to the date is labeled "To Whom Paid." Place the name of the company that provided the service in this box. For example, if you are writing up a taxi receipt, you would write the name of the taxi, not the name of the PA who gave you the receipt. Moving across the page, you will encounter a box entitled "Purpose." Write down the reason for the purchase. The purpose can be anything; safety rides, medicine for actors, etc. Petty cash can be used for anything as long as you have proper approval. The last box that you will need to fill out is the amount that was paid to the vendor. Repeat this procedure on every line of the PC envelope until you are finished. Once the front part of the envelope is filled out completely, stuff the taped receipts inside and send it off to the Accounting Department. You have successfully filled out a PC envelope. But what happens once it leaves your hands?

WHAT HAPPENS NOW?

The PC envelope arrives at the office where it is turned in to the Accounting Department. Accountants review the receipts and calculate the amount owed for each receipt. Once the tally has been approved, the envelope must be signed and approved by the head accountant and the unit production manager (UPM). Once these two sign off on your petty cash, the money will be counted, released, and sent to set with a distro run. When the money arrives on-set it will be attached to the front of your PC envelope. Count your money and make sure the amount is correct. On the top right corner of the envelope is a box that reads, "Received by:" with a space for a signature. Sign the envelope to confirm that you've received your petty cash. At the end of the day, any overages come out of your pocket.

TIPS AND THINGS TO KNOW

THINGS TO KNOW BEFORE YOU GET TO SET

Never Be without Toner

Never be without toner and ink for each printer and copier on-set. I was once working on a movie where the office sent me a big hunking copy machine. The heavy one that jams every minute or two... that's the one. So as any crewmember on-set can tell you, production burns through a lot of copies. The call sheet alone is 50 to 100 double-sided copies printed every day. Inevitably, your printer or copy machine will run out of ink and toner... and it will not take long. Now, I consider myself a good PA. I think ahead, I order things before they're needed. And this time was no exception. I had ordered backup toner about a week before this point. I never followed up on their arrival, I just assumed they were coming and forgot. Until that fateful day when in the middle of running the call sheet... the toner runs empty. No more toner = no more copies; no more copies = more trips to Kinko's. I called the production office now to follow up. Apparently, when I told the Office PA what I needed, she never passed the message on to the person who does the actual ordering. I should've called the secretary.

PREP

Before production starts... before you even set foot on a set... the ADs have been in preparation (prep) for at least three to six weeks. They have been planning, scheduling, organizing, and meeting with every department involved in production. Not everyone on the team will be needed during prep, but a few key players will be involved.

Prep will usually consist of five stages for a PA. The first parts of prep are made up of the fittings and the screen tests (see next). After these happen, prep moves into rehearsal times. In addition to the rehearsals, small shooting units may go out to capture any B-footage or small, special shots that can be sneaked in before production begins. Finally, you will have to do your physical prep for the shoot depending on which staff position you have been offered.

● FITTINGS & SCREEN TESTS

Fittings and screen tests require a very small crew. This crew can be made up of the camera team: camera operators, the Director of Photography, the 1st Assistant Cameraman, the 2nd Assistant Cameraman, the loader, and the Wardrobe Department. Then add a supervisor and one or two dressers, the principal hairstylist and makeup artist, and one or two Assistant Directors. For some screen tests, the gaffer, an electrician, and the Key Grip may be in attendance. From the PA world, you will be represented by the Key PA and the 1st Team (principal actors) PA. Again, some screen tests will require more help than others; the staff will fluctuate based on the needs of production.

Remember to treat a screen test like a regular shooting day. The Key PA's job is to facilitate and communicate the running of the set. His main purpose at a screen test is to keep the doors locked up for privacy and to keep the noise levels down for focus. Other than these two responsibilities, the Key PA is an extra hand there to help when needed.

While working on *The Beaver*, I was doing a screen test in White Plains, New York. The room that we were shooting in was large, with lots of windows, and echoey. Not an ideal situation when you want privacy and quiet. Since the only PAs in the room were the Key PA and myself, we had to lockup this entire room with four points of entry and windows on three sides. Simple, right? Each of us covered two doors and tried to stay vigilant... that is, until the gardening crew showed up to trim the hedges. After a brief negotiation, they agreed to return later to finish their work. It just goes to show, you never know when an issue will come up: Always be prepared.

Along with locking up the set, the Key PA will help to load equipment and act as the craft service representative for the day. Aside from the Key and an additional PA, the 1st Team PA will also be present to assist with the actors.

The 1st Team PA will run 1st Team during the screen tests. Again, treat this like a normal shooting day. Once the actors arrive you should make them comfortable and get them into Hair, Makeup, and Wardrobe. Chat with the department heads ahead of time so you have a game plan for getting the actors ready. Once the actors are camera-ready, find out if the ADs are ready on-set. When the time comes, you can walk the actors to their spot and stand by in case they need anything. At this point, if there are no other actors that need to be prepped, you may want to offer yourself to the Key as an additional body for lockups.... Once the test is finished, walk the actors back to the changing area and explain to them what will happen next. Now repeat this process until all tests are complete. And, just like every other day, you will need to fill out an Exhibit G.

The camera tests are important for a PA because they give you the opportunity to get to know the actors and key crewmembers before production begins. With this knowledge it's easier to facilitate a smooth start-up during principal photography.

Wardrobe fittings occur around the same time as the camera tests. Fittings can range in time from minutes to hours, depending on the costume. They will take place in the Wardrobe Department at the production office unless an actor specifically requests the fittings be held at another location, such as a residence.

If the fittings are at the production office, the 1st Team PA may be called in to coordinate the fittings and entertain the actors. On occasion the ADs will handle the fitting themselves, but on a day with multiple fittings, an extra hand can be a huge help.

• REHEARSALS AND PREP SHOOTS

Rehearsals are an integral part of the pre-production process for the actors, the Director of Photography, and the director. This is the time when they flesh out all of their questions about the script and attempt to block (establish the movement of actors) the harder scenes that will need to be shot. Rehearsals may take place at the director's home, or at a rented space. Wherever they may be, a PA might be asked to come in and oversee the rehearsal. The PAs that are often used for this task are the Key PA and the 1st Team PA. They will come in ahead of time to clean and set up the tables and chairs for the rehearsal. Once this is done, they'll lay out scripts, pencils, and notepads. The final thing that needs to be done during setup is to lay out the snacks and drinks for the rehearsal. Make sure that they are in a neat and orderly layout: Nothing says poor form like disorganized Crafty.

Once everything is set up, the PA in charge will wait for actors to arrive and direct them to the appropriate space for rehearsal. After rehearsal, the PA stays to help clean up before going home. This is by far one of the easiest days of prep you will encounter.

Small shooting units can be some of the most fun or the hardest days that you will encounter. During prep on one movie, I was sent out with the crew to a roller coaster at Rye Playland. The goal was to shoot the lead actors riding in the front seat of the roller coaster, having a great time and enjoying life. As we got to the park I saw that it was closed. We were the only ones allowed in. As the van pulled up to the roller coaster to unload, I noticed two other vans landing behind us. I stepped out of my van and was greeted by roughly three-quarters of the production office. They had all turned out to the park to ride the roller coaster and be in the movie! What a treat! So we had our little field trip, which lasted for about an hour, and then returned to the office for the rest of the day. This was an awesomely fun prep day.

Sometimes before principal photography begins, a small unit will go out and shoot stock footage or scenes with no dialogue. These prep days should be treated more like a real shoot than anything else we've discussed. Yes, the shoot will be more relaxed, but that doesn't mean that you can let your PA guard down. Days like this will require two or three PAs. The Key PA or a strong staffer will work on the team during these types of days. Like with the screen tests, the Key PA will help run the set, while the 1st Team PA prepares the actors. For the first time during prep, a Background PA may be asked to step in and help with signing in and setting (positioning) the background actors if necessary. Normally before production, small units are not big enough to warrant background and the like, but it's always good to be prepared. The Background PA is there to help with vouchers and stand-ins during the shoot. If the PA is on top of her responsibilities, she'll be free to help the Key PA with lockups. In certain cases, a Paperwork PA will be hired for this day as an additional hand and to put together a production report, since film stock will be shot.

One movie had me shooting a small unit on the Brooklyn Bridge in December. If you've ever been there, it's windy and freezing. As the only PA on this unit — shooting an actor riding his bike down the bridge walkway — I had to keep pedestrians out of our shot while fighting to hold a bounce card (white foam board used to reflect light) against the prevailing winds. It was a tough, exhausting day that wore me out completely. It was just a small unit, but remember, these small units can be hard, serious work. Bring your A-game and don't let the ADs think you're taking the job too lightly.

● *WALKIE PREP*

After all of the production prep, there are still one or two days of physical prep for the Walkie PA and the Paperwork PA.

The Walkie PA will come into the office one or two days before production is scheduled to start. During his prep time, the Walkie PA will receive his package from the rental house. The package must be thoroughly inventoried.

● *INVENTORY THE WALKIE PACKAGE*

To inventory the package, follow these simple steps:

1. Count all walkies and record all identification numbers on an inventory sheet (or on any paper, from which you will later transfer the numbers to a printed inventory sheet). The identification numbers can be found on the front of the walkie or on the inside of the walkie under the battery.
2. Count and total all of the spare batteries in the package.
3. Count and total all accessories (headsets, chargers, etc.).

Once the package has been inventoried, create a true inventory sheet. The columns should read like this:

Walkie #	Department	Crew Member	Signout Date	Accessories	Signature
	Camera				
693	Camera			☐ Survy ☐ BK ☐ Hand Mic	
1649	Camera			☐ Survy ☐ BK ☐ Hand Mic	
1652	Camera			☐ Survy ☐ BK ☐ Hand Mic	
1815	Camera			☐ Survy ☐ BK ☐ Hand Mic	
1884	Camera			☐ Survy ☐ BK ☐ Hand Mic	
	Grips				
1204	Grips			☐ Survy ☐ BK ☐ Hand Mic	
1218	Grips			☐ Survy ☐ BK ☐ Hand Mic	
1545	Grips			☐ Survy ☐ BK ☐ Hand Mic	
1737	Grips			☐ Survy ☐ BK ☐ Hand Mic	
1830	Grips			☐ Survy ☐ BK ☐ Hand Mic	
1843	Grips			☐ Survy ☐ BK ☐ Hand Mic	

● *DIVIDING UP THE PACKAGE*

Now that the inventory sheet is prepared, the Walkie PA will begin to divide up the walkies by department. There are many ways to pass out walkies to the crew. My preferred method involves paper bags that you can get from any local grocer.

Talk to the department heads in the office or check the crew list to get an idea of how many walkies each department will need. To prep the paper bags you simply need a Sharpie. On the front of the bag, write down the name of the department receiving the walkies. Next to the department name, write down the number of walkies in the bag and circle that number. Below this write down the quantity and type of accessories that have been placed in the bag. Now fill the bag with the appropriate equipment and be ready to pass it out on the first day. Be sure that you've recorded which department your walkies have been given to on your inventory sheet. Another method that I have seen is just as simple, but doesn't use the bags as identifiers. Instead, when grouping walkies, the Walkie PA will use different colors of tape to indicate a department. For example, green tape wrapped around a walkie antennae represents the Electric Department. Yellow tape on an antennae may represent the grips, and so on. Combining the two methods allows you to hand out and retrieve walkies quickly using the bag method while being able to easily identify walkies for inventory checks using the tape method.

Both of these methods work, or you can develop your own system. The goal is to be well organized so you will have less work to do later on. If a walkie goes missing, you'll have to hunt it down.

After the package has been fully prepared for set, it will be loaded onto a truck or a Teamster van to be delivered to set on Day One. The Walkie PA's prep day will be anywhere from six to twelve hours of work, depending on what you are asked to do. It's an easy day, so relax and enjoy it. The fun will start soon!

● *PAPERWORK PREP*

For the Paperwork PA, prep is a completely different experience. It can be long and tedious at times, but it's a good chance to get to know the people in the office. Paperwork PAs will get two days of prep. The reason for this... there's more to do. (Not really, if you do things right). Day One consists of physical prep and setting up all the paperwork that a PA will need on-set. Day Two is more about finishing whatever you did not get to the day before and holding meetings with the Accounting Department and the UPM.

MEET THE OFFICE

On the first day of prep I come into the office with a big smile on my face. For the first 30 minutes it's all about handshakes and introductions. Who are you and what are you doing here? This is your time to get to know the office and create a relationship that will stay with you for the run of the project. I like to introduce myself to everybody. This includes the janitors and the deliverymen. You never know who can help you out in a time of need. By making this my first act in the office, I come off as friendly (I really am), eager, and enthusiastic, while getting a chance to learn everyone's name and face. Once the rounds have been made, it's time to head over to the production office and chat with the Assistant Directors. It is best to have this chat as early as possible so that you will be aware of the AD's likes and dislikes. Every AD likes things done differently and prep is your time to figure out how to work best with your team. After this opening conversation, I move on to the real prep work.

ORDERING SUPPLIES

During my conversation with the ADs, I have asked them what types of pens and supplies they prefer. What type of printer ink does the 2nd AD need? Ask these questions now so that you can order everything that will be needed ahead of time. Once I have these answers I draw up a supply list. A list of supplies can be found in Appendix B of this book. Some supplies you will need that are not on the list include: a small medical kit, paperwork boxes with closable lids, and a production tin (a clipboard with a storage space inside) if you don't already have one. Once I have assembled my list, I type it up and hand it to the production secretary. For good measure, I will also email it. I know this sounds redundant, but the more you work, the more you will learn that this business is all about covering yourself and staying ahead. Once I send off the email, my supply time has expired and I must move on to the task of building an AD kit.

● *BUILDING THE AD KIT*

Building an AD kit is the tedious part of prep that I alluded to earlier. It is one of those painstaking arts and crafts projects that you will be thankful you did, once it's completed. The kit stores every piece of paperwork that will be needed on-set during the course of production, so try to organize it in a way that is easy for other people to understand.

To start, you will have to find a box. But not just any box. This box must accommodate legal-size paper and have a lip on the edge for hanging file folders. It must also have a lid to protect the paperwork from the elements.

The box has been found and it is now time to start filling it. The office will have legal-size hanging folders available. Grab about 30 of them to start off with. Once the folders are in the box, you have come to the task of labeling them. Each label should be written clearly so anyone searching your kit can identify what they are looking for. The way in which you organize your kit is a personal preference. For a full list of paperwork that will be needed for the kit, refer to Appendix B of this book.

I like to start my kit by dividing it into four separate sections. I use bigger tabs or manila folders to indicate a break between each of these sections.

The first section is always the "PROJECT" section. This section contains all of the information that you will need to understand what is happening with the project. Paperwork in this section includes scripts, schedules, one-liners, etc. This section is constantly being updated and revised, so make sure to keep up with the current drafts. I always throw out the old paperwork when revisions come in, but keep one copy of all previous drafts in case they need to be referred to.

Behind the project section you will find the "CREW PAPER-WORK" section. This section is rather sparse, containing only accident reports. It's a good way to set them apart in case you need them later.

The third section is very important. This is the "ACCOUNTING" section. Home to some of the most useful paperwork on-set, this is the section that gets you paid. It holds start work, time cards, box-kit rentals, and petty cash requests, just to name a few items. This section will get the most use and the most snooping of any other paperwork in your kit, so be sure that all of the paperwork is well-stocked.

The last section that you will create is the "PRODUCTION" section. It contains copies of all of the paperwork that a PA and an AD will need to do their respective jobs on-set. This is where the 1st Team PA will go to get Exhibit Gs, and the Background PA will go for the background breakdown. This section also contains copies of all maps, directions, and skins (list of the names and roles of all background actors) that have been collected to date. Production will eat through this paperwork like termites on balsa, so again, make sure that you are keeping up with the kits.

Finally, we have our AD kit together. By this point, the sun will probably be setting and your eyes will be red from staring at labels all day. It's probably time to go home. Ask your ADs if there is anything else that you can do for them. If no, enjoy the short day. You won't get many more.

STARTING DAY TWO

Hello! You came back for Day Two, welcome! Most of the organizing was done yesterday so now it's time for the logistics. The two big meetings that you will have on this day are with Accounting and the UPM. If these people are unavailable, you will have time to finish anything you didn't get to yesterday. Just stay busy so it doesn't look like you're being paid to sit around.

● *MEETING WITH ACCOUNTING*

The first meeting that you will be able to take is probably the one with the Accounting Department. The meeting takes between 10 and 30 minutes from start to finish and is attended by two or three people. The first person is the Head Accountant. With him you will discuss the process for petty cash, and what the pay scales are for additionals. After this meeting, you will sit down with the Payroll Accountant. This is one of the most important parts of prep because it relates directly to the time cards and the PRs.

In your meeting with the Payroll Accountant, you will ask how he prefers the way the time cards are filled out. The accountant will tell you which day is the week-ending day, what the rates are, and the proper way to fill out comments and indicate times on your time card (i.e., standard time or military time). These two meetings can be taken almost any time throughout the day, so I prefer to try for the unit production manager first, if possible.

● *MEETING WITH THE UPM*

The Unit Production Manager is the top dog in your world. He is also one of the busiest people in the office. The UPM is constantly on the phone chatting with anyone involved with the production. Because he is so busy, it is best to prime him in the morning by asking for the meeting, and then returning after a few hours to follow up. Don't be pushy, and don't be scared. If he is not available, find something else to do and come back later.

When he has a moment to squeeze you in between phone calls, make your presentation quick and concise. Most of the questions that you have will be about rules and preferences. This meeting will take about 10 to 25 minutes and should be very fast-paced. Have your questions in front of you as the UPM will not lead this meeting. The more prepared you are, the better this meeting will go.

A list of questions for the accountants and the UPM can be found in Appendix B of this book. Now that our AD kit is prepped and our meetings are finished, it's time to work on negotiating your deal as a PA.

• *NEGOTIATE YOUR DEAL*

When you sit down with the UPM, ask questions about your rate. When do Paperwork PAs get overtime? Are you using your computer on-set? Make sure that you get a kit-rental for your computer. Do you use your cell phone on-set more often than anyone in your department? You may be entitled to a cell phone allowance. This meeting with the UPM is time to figure out how everything will work, and nail down your deal as a Paperwork PA. Don't be afraid to negotiate; the worst thing they can say is no.

• *ORGANIZING YOUR SUPPLIES*

For those of you who like being Boy Scouts, there is one other task that can occupy your prep days: building an organized supply kit. I like to use a fishing tackle box with pull-out drawers. It holds all of my office supplies and is extremely portable. The way in which you organize your kit is completely up to you. I only stock it with the supplies that I use most: pens, pencils, Sharpies, paperclips, sticky notes, tape, staplers, etc. Check your supply list and figure out what you'll need to keep close and what will fit in the kit. Different productions will go through different supplies. As you work you will learn to anticipate who uses what supplies and how often they will need to be restocked. On heavy background jobs you know you'll need paperclips and sticky notes. On heavy 1st Team jobs, be ready with a lot of pens.

If you've finished this, it's time for the final act of prep, the load-out. You will most likely be the only PA in the office at this point, so it becomes your job to load any equipment that will be needed on-set into a Teamster van or truck for transport. It's not the best way to end prep, but it is time to pat yourself on the back because you've probably only got one day off before shooting begins.

HOW TO READ A SCRIPT

I know, I know, you went to school already. You know how to read, it all makes sense. But why is it spaced so funny? What are all of the stars and numbers on the page? Scripts are designed so that they are easy to read and understand. The pages are spaced to keep from jumbling up information and all notations are a means of tracking changes, scenes, and lines. So, did you know that? If so, you're ahead of the game. If not, keep reading.

Scripts are created to be easily broken down into elements. An element is any aspect of the production (talent, special equipment, props, makeup, F/X, etc.). Breaking a script into its elements is actually the basic foundation of an AD's job. The script contains most of the information that will be used to create the schedule and drive the production forward. In this section I will examine the structure of a scene in a script.

Centered at the top of the script page you will find the title of the project and the current revision color. Script revisions are printed on a different color of paper so that changes can be clearly seen. Scripts are printed in the following color order: white, blue, pink, yellow, green, and an odd color (Salmon, Rose, or Sea Foam Green). If more revisions are needed, scripts are printed in the doubles round: When all the colors have been used, further rounds are labeled "Doubles" and start over at the first color — white — then blue, pink, and through the cycle again. Television episodes will go through many more revisions than feature films do. To the right of this centered heading you will find the script page number.

● *THE SCENE HEADING*

After finding the page you wish to read in the correct revision of your script, it's time to look at the building blocks. Scripts are made up of scenes and each scene begins with a heading.

32   INT COWBOY'S ROOFTOP - DAWN   32

The heading gives you four pieces of information. First, it tells you the scene number for easy reference. The first script that is released does not usually have scene numbers. They are assigned by the UPM or the ADs when breaking everything down. The second part of the heading lets you know whether the scene takes place indoors (INTerior) or outdoors (EXTerior). The next piece of the heading describes the location where the scene takes place. This does not constitute a real-life location. A rooftop set can easily be shot on a soundstage. I once shot a movie where a man jumps 60 feet off a balcony, but the balcony was only 5 feet off the ground inside a warehouse in Brooklyn. The last piece of the heading tells you the time of day within the world of the script. This particular scene takes place at dawn. The time of day is important because it affects the lighting of the scene and the equipment needed. This in turn affects the setup time and the schedule. See! It's all connected. Below the scene heading is the action section.

● *THE ACTION SECTION*

32   INT   COWBOY'S ROOFTOP - DAWN   32

Dolly up to the roof to reveal COWBOY leaning against the chimney in the rain. His best friend JOAN climbs onto the roof holding a baseball bat. Cowboy hears her approach from behind, but not turn around.

In the action section, you will learn what the characters are physically doing in the scene. This can be considered the setup phase. It will describe camera movements, location descriptions, character descriptions, and any physical action that happens in the story. No story is complete without some form of communication. The section that follows the action portion is the dialogue section.

● *THE DIALOGUE SECTION*

The dialogue section contains the character names, the type of dialogue spoken, and the spoken words themselves.

The character names are centered on the page and written in all capital letters. To the right of the character name you may find two letters, O.S. or V.O. These indicate the type of dialogue being spoken in the script. If there are no letters next to the character name, the words are spoken by the characters as written. O.S. stands for off-screen lines. These are lines spoken in the scene, but the speaker is not seen by the camera. An example of this is someone calling to a friend in another room. The friend's reply would be considered off-screen dialogue. V.O. stands for voice over. This is dialogue that will be recorded separately from the picture and then played over an edited scene. These words are never spoken aloud on camera.

32   INT COWBOY'S ROOFTOP - DAWN   32

Dolly up to the roof to reveal COWBOY leaning against
the chimney in the rain. His best friend JOAN climbs
onto the roof holding a baseball bat. Cowboy hears her
approach from behind, but not turn around.

JOAN (O.S.)

You OK?
COWBOY

Fine, did you finish it?

Joan lifts the bat, eyeing the bloody tip. She steps closer
to Cowboy as she raises the bat to swing.

JOAN (V.O.)

Almost...

The most common use of a voice over is as a narration. Below
the character name and type of dialogue you will find the character's
dialogue. When combined, these form a coherent conversation that
will lead to screenings at festivals, invitations to award ceremonies,
and that long walk to the winners' podium.

Understanding how to read a script is an important skill for a PA
to have. If you can pick out the major details in each section, you
will be able to better prepare for your job.

● READING BETWEEN THE LINES — THE KEY PA

For a Key PA, the description of the scene and some camera movement gives him an idea of where to set PA lockups. A description
of the action tells the Key to look out for certain safety hazards. In
a scene on the roof, we know it is dangerous to be on an elevated
platform. It's even more dangerous to be on one that is slanted and

wet with rain. Having read the scene ahead of time, the Key will know that an actor must walk a path across this wet roof and that this path must be both safe and clear of people and objects.

● *READING BETWEEN THE LINES — THE BACKGROUND PA*

For a Background PA, the script gives her an idea of how many extras will be needed for each scene. In our scene on the roof we only have two principal actors. Two principal actors calls for the use of two extras (stand-ins). If the scene were to take place inside a dance bar, the Background PA could assume she'll be working with a bartender, at least five bar patrons, and maybe a bus boy or two. Reading the scene beforehand will not only prepare you as PA, it will help you assist the AD when setting the background actors on-set. Don't overstep your bounds, but be prepared to offer creative input if asked.

● *READING BETWEEN THE LINES — THE 1st TEAM PA*

The 1st Team PA will look at the script to see which principal actors will be needed for each scene. Aside from the topical information, it is important for the 1st Team PA to read the script because he spends a lot of time with the actors. Sometimes actors like to discuss scenes or run lines (rehearse) while they wait to be called to set. At other times, reading the script will clue a PA in to the mood of an actor. Knowing what type of state an actor is trying to put himself in can be invaluable when navigating the political waters of 1st Team. For instance, you wouldn't want to smile and high five an actress who is about to perform a scene in which she learns of her son's death. (Yes... I did it and I'm not proud of it.) Reading the script will help you relate to what the actors are trying to do and give you a better insight into how to treat them properly.

Who wants to go to work blind? The script is the plan that production will follow on its path of creation. You now understand how to read a script; my challenge to you is to now look beyond the page. Take what you've learned from this book and try to anticipate the needs of production according to the words on the page. I promise you will become a stronger PA.

● *NOTES ABOUT SCRIPT REVISIONS*

Earlier we talked about script changes and revisions. Before a script goes into production, it will be finalized. This means that no more changes can be made to the first draft. From this point forward all changes are considered revisions. Whenever this happens, there are ways of marking the changes in the script. Use this list of rules to understand how a script goes through revisions:

1. Script revisions come in two sizes: full script revisions and revised script pages. If 70% or more of a script has been revised, it's time for a full script revision. Anything less than that is simple page revisions.

2. Any changes made to the script after it has been locked will be marked with an asterisk (*) on the left and right margins of the changed lines.

3. To add scenes to a locked script, the added scene is assigned a number paired with a letter. For example, to add a scene between 32 and 33, you would write scene 32A.

4. Sometimes when a scene is added, it will spill over onto another page. This new page will contain only the spillover from the added scene. To indicate an added page in a locked script, pair a letter with the page number the same way we did with the added scene in rule 3.

5. When a scene is removed from a locked script it must still be accounted for. In place of the scene on the page, you will simply find the scene number and the word "OMITTED" as a scene heading.

6. If an entire page or series of pages is removed from a revision, the gap is noted by labeling the pages missing with a hyphenated number. For example, if we were to delete pages 45, 46, and 47 from our script, the revised script pages would read pages 43, 44–48, 49, etc.

THINGS TO KNOW ON-SET

EQUIPMENT & GEAR

Rule No. 1 for every PA is "be prepared." Meaning, while shooting in Central Park in December you do not wear shorts, a tank top, and tanning oil. (Yes, this actually happened.) You do need to think ahead. This means acquiring the proper gear for the weather, the terrain, and the daily functions that your particular job requires.

First we'll start with the basics. Any PA can tell you it sucks to be caught in the rain. Standing in soaked clothing for hours will make anyone a little upset. I was working on the movie *The Taking of Pelham 123* and we were on the Manhattan Bridge on a beautiful summer day. I wore shorts and a t-shirt and sat on the bridge for hours telling some background cops when to walk toward the camera. All of a sudden the sky opens up and I am soaked, nothing to save me but a garbage bag from Crafty. The next day I went out and bought a rain suit. It is simply rubber pants and a rubber raincoat that fits over your clothes. It'll keep you dry and prevent you from looking like a receptacle. You should also wear waterproof shoes or overshoes (essentially a rubber boot that fits over your shoes and keeps water out).

Make sure to check the weather report before you go to work and bring the appropriate weather gear. If you're shooting in snow, bundle up; if you're on the beach in 105-degree weather… don't bundle up.

Now for functioning gear. On any given Sunday anything can happen. That is a PA's Monday through Friday. You never know what you will need, so anticipate and learn to read people. Your gear is something you should carry or have quick access to at a moment's notice.

- Things You Should Always Carry
— A pen, plus some extras
— Red, green, and black Sharpies
— Sides
— Something to write on
— An extra walkie battery

— Gum and/or mints
— At least one bottle of water
— A lighter and a book of matches
— Walkie talkie, headset
  • Things You Should Have Nearby
— Extra napkins/tissues
— Paper clips
— Good book or crossword puzzle (only if you are stuck in Holding)
— Sticky notes

Carry these few items and you should be well on your way to becoming a great PA. They'll at least help you get started while you figure out what you will need to carry for each gig.

SHOTS

Every good PA should know the names of the different types of shots. Here are a few labels to at least get you acclimated to what you will hear on-set.

Abby — The Abby is the second-to-last shot of the night. It's named after Abby Singer, a 1st AD who would always the call the last shot of the night one scene early.

Dutch Angle — A shot that is tilted diagonally so the screen appears like it is slanting to one direction.

Martini — The very last shot of the night, also known as a "drinkable" shot or something you can put in a glass.

Oner — (pronounced won-er) A scene that can be completed in one shot.

Over (character name) onto (character name) — Usually a shot over one character's shoulder onto the face of another.

Raking — If a shot is raking it means that the camera will be moving sideways along a predetermined axis.

Reverse — The reverse angle of a shot that was just completed. The other perspective.

Two-shot — A shot with two actors on camera.

Walk and Talk — the camera follows actors as they walk through a scene holding a conversation.

THE TRUCKS

You can break the trucks into two categories: base camp and the working trucks.

Base camp consists of the honeywagon, star campers (trailers), the Wardrobe truck, and Hair and Makeup trailers:

● BASE CAMP

The Honeywagon: is a long trailer with lots of stairs. It houses the production office, the AD room, bathrooms, and small, cast dressing rooms.

The honeywagon is a large trailer that houses the production office, day player rooms, and bathrooms near set.

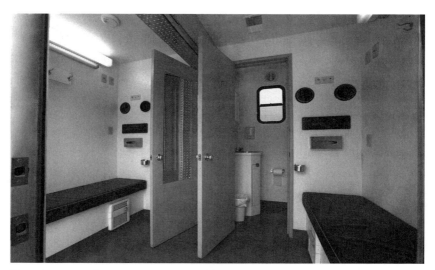

This is a honeywagon dressing room. *Courtesy of Haddad's, Inc.*

The Star Campers: have multiple names depending on the type of trailer. If only one star is in a large trailer, it is known as a star camper. If it has two rooms in it, the trailer is known as a two-banger. If the trailer has three rooms, it's a three-banger.

A single star camper. This trailer houses the lead actors or supporting leads on a film.

Lavishly equipped with a living room, dinette, bedroom, bathroom (with shower), and a kitchen, the star trailer becomes a second home.

A 2-banger houses two actors. It is similar to a star camper, but does not have the bedroom or the kitchen. Instead, it holds a pullout couch for resting. *Courtesy of Haddad's, Inc.*

The Hair & Makeup Trailer: Usually this is a trailer with two entrances on the same side of the trailer. It will have at least two windows and sometimes a bathroom. The trailer is equipped with mirrored stations, a sink, and a hair-washing basin (like you see in a salon). These two departments work in tandem and are always in or near each other.

The Hair and Makeup trailer looks like a normal truck with no back gate. Instead, it has a side entrance.

Each trailer is equipped with a wall of mirrors and Hair and Makeup stations for each artist working. *Courtesy of Haddad's, Inc.*

The Wardrobe Truck: The Wardrobe truck will most likely be the length of a honeywagon. It has two entrances. One is on the side of the truck near the front of the trailer and the second is at the back of the truck and usually has steps or a ramp. Inside this truck are racks for hanging clothes, drawers and shelves for storing fabric, thread, and the like, and a washer/dryer combo for those on-the-job accidents (cast only).

The wardrobe truck is a long truck with two entrances. A lift gate on the back and a staircase on the side; this is where production is supplied with all of its clothes.

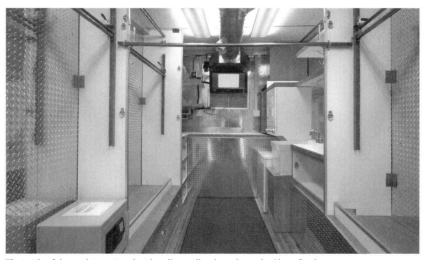

The inside of the truck is equipped with wall-to-wall racks and a washer/dryer for those messy actors on set. *Courtesy of Haddad's, Inc.*

Where do we come up with these names? I'm not sure about the bangers. I can only speculate. But the story I was told about the honeywagon was that the odor from the bathrooms became so rancid that bugs would swarm the area like bees to honey... hence the honeywagon.

● *THE WORKING TRUCKS*

The working trucks are straightforward. The Prop Department shares their truck with Scenic and set dressing. The Camera Department shares their truck with Sound. The grips and electrics each have their own truck, as well as one or two devoted stake-bed trucks to haul equipment from the working trucks to set.

The Prop Truck: This truck houses all of the props that will be needed on location. It also contains fans and heaters if actors get uncomfortable. The inside of the truck is lined with shelves and drawers for storage. If the Prop Department wasn't enough, this truck also houses the set dressing cart, usually equipped with a toolbox for quick fixes and repairs. The big boy of the group is the camera Scenic. While he may only have one cart, as a department of one he must carry around all of the paints and goops and brushes and papers and pens, etc. All of the Scenic's equipment is stored on the truck.

The Camera Truck: The camera truck can be identified by its plain black backdoors and its two entrances. The first entrance is on the back and will contain a liftgate, and the second entrance is on the side. The side door has a set of stairs and a sliding door for double security when working with exposed film. The inside of the truck is broken up into three main sections. The back half is storage and shelving, the front half is working counter space. Now I said three sections. There is a room inside the trailer with a separate door. This is the truck's darkroom, where all of the film is canned and loaded. The Camera Department shares this truck with the Sound Department. Sound does not usually take up much space as it consists of a mixing cart, a boom holder/pole, and two or three shelves for storage. Though you never know. I once worked on a movie where the Sound Department took up two-thirds of the storage space.

The camera truck has two entrances. A stair on the side and a lift gate on the back.

The inside of the camera truck is shared with sound. It contains shelves and cabinets as well as a workbench and a neat little darkroom for loading magazines with film. *Courtesy of Haddad's, Inc.*

The Grip Truck: Easily identified by checking the inside. If you see wooden boards and metal pipes, you've found it. The grip truck is simply a long trailer with a liftgate on the back. Its interior is divided into sections with racks, shelves, and drawers. The truck houses plywood and floorboards, 2 x 4 lumber, nuts, bolts, power tools, and more. To add to this, the truck also stores rolling carts stocked with equipment, dollies, and ladders.

The Electric Truck: Similar to the grip truck. The only difference is what's on the inside. On an electric truck you will find shelves and drawers for small items; on a grip truck you will find open space used for storing lights and light stands.

The grip and electric trucks are long box trucks with shelving that holds lights, cables, C-stands, and any other item a grip or electric may need. © *Joshua A. Friedman 2010.*

The Crafty Truck: Crafty will have one of two things. On some jobs they will have a rented van that stores all of the food, tables, and equipment that they use. On other jobs, you'll find a dedicated Crafty truck. This truck houses a working kitchen with stovetops, flattops, ovens, and grills. It has a refrigeration unit to keep the food cold and cabinets for storage. Outside, the truck has a side window and rear door, both with closing hatches. This unit is great for location shoots with large crews to feed.

The Crafty truck is a mobile kitchen and sometimes comes equipped with a serving window.

Inside the truck you will find a full kitchen with stovetops, refrigerators, etc. *Courtesy of Haddad's, Inc.*

Your job as a PA is to be able to identify every one of these trucks at a glance. You need this knowledge on the off chance that you have to run a script to the producer's two-banger room: You don't want it to end up in the Hair and Makeup trailer. Another reason to know about the trucks is because at the end of the night, your Key PA will invariably ask you to stand next to a department truck to hand out call sheets and list out-times. If you don't know which truck, be prepared to face the wrath of a crew without call sheets. Good luck!

COFFEE VS. CAPPUCCINO VS. LATTE

At some point in your PA career you will feel like you're becoming a barista. Don't worry, you won't need the two-week Starbuck's training course. PAs really only need to know how to make coffee three ways: in a cup, as a cappuccino, or as a latte. The process is simple and will score you major brownie points with the person who requested the coffee. Here's how to make it happen.

It is surprising to me how many people do not know how to use a coffee machine. Start by lining the inside of the top with a coffee filter. Depending on the type of coffee, place two or three scoops of ground coffee inside the filter. Place the filter with the coffee into the top of the machine; pour in water up to the top line of the machine's reservoir, and press the "on" button. The water will be heated and slowly dripped through the ground coffee. When all of the water has dripped through the filter, the coffee in the carafe is ready. Pour it into a cup, add cream and sugar as wanted, and serve.

Cappuccinos are a little more complicated than making straight coffee. To start, you will need an espresso machine, a steamer, and some milk. Step one involves pouring milk into a coffee cup about one third of the way. Once you have the correct amount of milk, stick the arm of the steamer into the milk and slowly move the cup around until the steam turns the milk frothy. It will start to bubble and foam on top. As soon as the milk is nice and foamy, put your cup under the pour spot and put one shot of espresso directly in the center of your foam. There will be a brown dollop in the middle of your white foam that lets you know that it's cappuccino. Add sugar if desired and enjoy.

Lattes are very similar to cappuccinos. They have the same ingredients, but different proportions. If cappuccinos are made of a shot of espresso and a little milk, then lattes are made with a shot of espresso and a lot of milk. As with the cappuccino, the first step is to foam the milk. For a latte, use a half a cup of milk or more. Once the milk is foamy, set it aside. Pour your espresso shot into a separate cup and pour the milk on top of it, using a spoon or knife to catch the foam before it slides away. The last step is to spoon the foam onto the top of your latte for that creamy first sip.

You now know how to make the three most common coffees requested on-set. Here's a fast way to distinguish them by their ingredients:

Coffee — Made of 100% dripped coffee, with cream or sugar added per request.

Cappuccino — Made of equal parts espresso, milk, and foam.

Latte — Made of a shot of espresso with a lot of milk on top and some foam.

GAMBLING ON-SET (NEVER HAPPENS...)

You'll spend a lot of time on-set with the same people. When this happens, life tends to get routine and boring. To avoid this downturn, production and other departments will come up with pools and games to play on-set. These games keep the crew distracted (in a good way, most of the time) and entertained, at least for a little while. Below I will share a few of the games we play on-set. Note: I in no way, shape, or form condone gambling on-set. Now it's your turn to deal.

● THE CARD GAME

The card game is simple. Once a week, usually on Friday, a PA (you) will go to the store and purchase two different colored decks of cards. The colors are important for later. When you arrive on-set open up the first deck and shuffle the cards. Once the cards are opened, the clock starts ticking; a PA now has until lunchtime to sell all 52 cards to the crew.

To sell the cards, a PA will walk around the set asking crewmembers if they would like to buy a card. The price of the cards will vary depending on how frugal the crew is, but most games sell cards for $10 or $20. If your card game will be more expensive than that, try to give the crew a few days notice so they know to bring more money for the big card game. On *Law & Order* we once sold $50 cards.

When selling the cards, remember that every person on the crew should have a chance to play. Whether they buy a card or not, offering a crewmember the chance to buy a card makes them feel like they're part of the team. I try to give the crew first shot at the cards because once you start selling cards to the Teamsters they disappear fast. Teamsters will buy two to four cards. That's great at the end of the selling period when you need to unload the remaining cards, but it's unfair to the rest of the crew who would like an opportunity to play. Once a crewmember has bought a card, he will keep it with him until the prize cards are drawn from the second deck. The drawing does not take place until all 52 cards are sold.

Set up the drawing in a public place. Hopefully, a trustworthy PA is running the card game and has asked the ADs if he can pull the cards before lunch. It is always a good idea to check with your AD before you do anything that may disrupt the flow of work on-set. Once you have approval, open the second deck, shuffle the cards, and lay them face down on a flat surface or in a box. Choose a random castmember or crewmember to draw three cards from the deck. The cards are picked in reverse order. The first card will be third prize, the second card will be second prize, and the third card drawn is first prize. Be sure to call the winning cards out clearly, both in person and on the walkie-talkie. Once crewmembers show you that they bought cards that match the cards drawn, it's time to pay up.

For a $10 card game, the prizes from highest to lowest will be $300, $150, and $70. If the cards are being sold for $20, those prizes will double. Regardless of the selling price of the cards, use these prize ratios as the basis for splitting the total pot. For instance, for a $50 card, first place would be $1,500, second place would be $750, and third place would be $350. Not a bad Friday haul.

The card game is a great way to give three crewmembers a bonus for the weekend. It's especially nice when the PAs win. Now, as PAs we do not make much money. Everyone understands that, so actors, producers, and some crewmembers will buy an extra card or two and donate it to the PAs. Be gracious, it's their way of showing appreciation, like tipping the dealer in blackjack. If you win, so do they; if you don't win, no harm, no foul.

The last aspect of the card game for a PA is the tip. Everyone hates asking for money, but we don't do this for free. The cards cost money, selling them takes time out of the day, and the PA with the cards is going to suffer a lot of ball-busting. To compensate the PA for his hard, hard work, the winners will tip about 10% of their winnings to the PA who runs the card game. Some people just don't know that they are supposed to tip; gently and respectfully remind them. Or if you're not into confrontation, mention this to someone else who you know will say something later. Either way, you'll be taken care of.

● *THE BUCKET*

For long-term jobs, a bucket may be a great way to get the crew involved. This had better be a pretty special bucket to affect a crew in this way, and it is. The concept of the bucket is very straightforward. Find an empty five-gallon plastic jug like the ones on the water coolers in an office. If you can't find one, check with Crafty. Tape the mouth of the bottle with duct tape or gaff tape and cut a slit wide enough to allow dollar bills into the bucket, but nothing else. Now go out and find yourself a chain, a lock, and some Sharpies. The prep work has just been done.

If you're feeling artsy, decorate the bottle with your Sharpies or magazine cutouts. When you're happy with the look of your bottle, place it in a public place where the crew will see it. Crafty is usually a good choice since it draws the most foot traffic. Once you have chosen a spot, use the lock and chain to secure the bottle to a solid object. We don't want our money walking away, now do we? On the outside of the bottle write in big letters the words "$5 BUCKET." Now I should explain the instructions.

Take a $5 bill and write your name on it in pen or Sharpie. Now drop the bill into the bucket. That's all. Crewmembers can drop as many bills in the bucket as they want to. This is a long-term game because it takes some time to build up a nice winning pot. It also gives the crew something to look forward to in the future: Someone will be walking home with a fat wad of fives. Usually towards the end of a job, a bucket drawing is held. A crewmember will saw off the top of the water-cooler jug, reach in and grab one or two bills. The number of winners is determined before the drawing begins so that the person pulling the bills will know how many to reach for. The winning names are read aloud and the money is divided and awarded. Another successful game. Did you get your tip?

● *BINGO*

Bingo can be one of the most exciting games to play on-set. To pull it off, you will have to go out and buy a bingo set, but don't fret. It pays for itself after one game and you can then enjoy it with your fellow PAs forever. Like the card game, bingo involves walking around to crewmembers and selling cards. This time, instead of selling playing cards, you are selling bingo cards. Each card will sell for $5 or $10. Once enough cards have been sold to allow for a decent size prize, the game will begin.

Playing bingo on-set can be a challenge. It's best to only use this game when you know that you will be in one location for an entire shooting day, and when you know that you will shoot one scene that takes at least half the day. On days like this, the crew tends to become bored and antsy. Playing bingo distracts them from that antsy feeling so that they can stay more focused during those long drawn-out takes.

Every twenty or thirty minutes, roll the bingo ball and call out a number. Make sure that PAs are echoing the bingo numbers so that all crewmembers can keep up. The game will continue for a few hours or until someone calls bingo. At this point, confirm the win, pay up, and wait for everyone who lost to start throwing their cards at you. I'll bet this one made the day go by faster.

● *THE WRAP GAME*

PAs should know everything about what is going on in the world of the set. Our job is to facilitate the day's work and help keep production on schedule. Out of this duty to stay on schedule, a friendly wager can be made. This wager will involve ADs, some PAs, and sometimes the Director of Photography and/or gaffer. This is a friendly wager for a nominal amount of money (usually $20 to $50) that can make the end of the day very exciting.

All you have to do is guess what time the camera will wrap. Whoever guesses the closest without going over the time wins the bet for that day. This game isn't very widespread, and PAs often won't play, but I like a challenge and enjoy this one because I have to use my knowledge of the shooting day to determine the estimated wrap time. There is no big prize in this game other than bragging rights, but sometimes that is enough!

As I said in the beginning of this section, I do not condone gambling on-set of any kind. But my boss tells me it can be a great morale booster.

HOW TO GET A JOB

Back-to-Back Jobs

I'm admittedly a workaholic. I can't get enough of what I do for a living. So when I first started in this industry, I would take any job that was offered to me. My longest straight workweek was 13 days long. It happened like this.

I was a staff PA on *Law & Order* during the week. Monday through Friday my work schedule included roughly 80 hours of work. I received a phone call Thursday night to see if I could work an overnight shoot on Saturday for the movie *Hancock*. Of course I said yes, there was plenty of time between the end of my Friday night shoot and a night shoot on Saturday. I went to work at 7:00 p.m. for the movie. At 8:00 p.m. I got a call to see if I could work the following day on the movie *The Taking of Pelham 123*. Again I said yes. I worked on *Hancock* until 6:00 a.m. Sunday morning before grabbing a taxi and running over to *Pelham 123*. I spent a 14-hour day working that job before heading home to grab a few hours of sleep. I woke up at 4:00 a.m. in time to get to work for another week on *Law & Order*. After the end of my long workweek, all I could do was crash. I had pushed myself to the limit by working non-stop. Take a break... there will always be more work.

TYPES OF JOBS

There are different types of jobs that you could work on during the course of your career. Some people prefer feature films, both independent (indies) and studio. Some prefer a life filled with episodic television and commercials. Still others choose to work on short projects, music videos, and industrials (educational tapes, training videos, and business presentations). Each type of job has its own drawbacks and advantages. Knowing how each job works will help you in discovering your career path and understanding which part of the industry you would prefer to work in.

FEATURE FILMS

Feature films are full-length projects (over 60 minutes) that tell a definitive story. Projects can last from 14 days to a few years, depending on their magnitude. The film *Saw* was shot in 16 days while *The Lord of the Rings* movies took years to shoot. Bigger talent is attached to feature films, which offer more money in a shorter amount of time.

Studio features may be the big budget blockbusters you see every summer, or the small indie hit that came from a first-time director. The budgets range from $5 million to over $400 million. These projects are strictly run and watched over by the producing studio.

An alternative to a studio feature is an independent feature. Independent features have smaller budgets and tend to be more creative in their problem-solving techniques. Most crewmembers on independent projects are there because they love to be involved in the art of filmmaking. At the same time, some of the non-union people on these jobs have little understanding of what they should be doing. There are plusses and minuses to both types of productions.

Feature films will present a PA with more challenges. The job is always different and it's easier to stay interested in the tasks at hand. On a feature, the schedule is a little slower. The page count gets smaller and the shot list gets larger. Feature films must also allow for more set-up time between shots because of the many angles a director may want. Another advantage for working in feature films is the hours. You will work more hours (and in turn make more money). Features will pay higher overtime rates than television shows because they are on a tighter schedule. Hours (in spite of the money) can also be a major drawback to feature films. I once worked a 22-hour day on a feature in which we shot one scene that was three-eighths of a page long.

If you are the type of person who likes constant change, features offer great short-term employment. The job will last long enough for you to make a few friends, and not too many enemies, before shoving off to the unemployment line or taking your next gig. PAs who only work on features are constantly searching for their next gig. It's a lifestyle that ends up being lived paycheck to paycheck.

EPISODIC TELEVISION

Episodic television shows vary in length from 30 minutes to 60 minutes. Each episode tells a piece of a story that weaves through-out the entire run of the series. Episodes take between 4 and 16 days to shoot on average, depending on the type of show. A 30-minute sitcom will shoot four days a week while a 60-minute procedural show will average eight days of shooting. The draw of television is in the stability of the work offered.

For a PA looking to gain some quick experience or some fast qualifying days for membership in the Directors Guild of America (DGA), television is the medium you want. Seasons last from three to eight months, with breaks for holidays and hiatuses. It's nice to know that you'll have a steady paycheck coming for a few months. Some productions also offer health insurance.

Most television shows are run by a network. It is the equivalent of a studio running a feature. The network constantly checks up to make sure that everything is on schedule and under budget. The good thing about working for a network is that they protect you as an employee. Network shows will try to stay within a 16-hour workday. If they go over this the costs start to rise very quickly. Feature films are better equipped to handle this kind of workday because they plan for it in the budget and schedule. An alternate reason for keeping the day under 16 hours is to save your crew from burning out. When you work those hours for five days straight and sleep less than eight hours per night, you will have to crash in order to function. As a PA it's your job to take good care of your body before *you* cease to function.

Another potential drawback to working in television is the monotony of the day. Many shows break their schedule up into studio days and location days. The average episode allows for three days in the studio and five days on location. In the studio, there is nowhere for a PA to go during times when there is no work to do. Doing the same thing, in the same place, with the same people for months at a time, does start to take its toll on you. A show's season may end before you are too irritated by anyone on-set, but be aware that crew tempers may run high and adjust your temperament to deal with the situation.

Episodic television can be lots of fun. Remember I said that you might get irritated by other crewmembers on-set after being with them for months at a time? There is a reason for this. People in episodic television become your family. You see them for at least 14 hours, five days every week for months at a time. A PA doesn't even see his roommate that often. These relationships are strong and can really help you learn your craft and be part of the collaborative effort. Seeing as how this clan of artisans has now become your family, I feel it is completely appropriate that they irritate you from time to time.

COMMERCIALS

Commercials vary in length by increments of 15 seconds. The shortest commercial I have ever seen was 15 seconds long, while the longest was over 2 minutes. They are designed to advertise a product or a service, and require all of the same elements as a larger project. Commercial shoots last from one to four days on average and move very fast. One of the best parts about commercials is the rate.

The rate on a commercial is $200 or more for a full day of work. The rate is higher than on features and TV shows because you are asked to do more work. On union jobs, a PA cannot touch equipment unless he is in the union authorized to touch it. On a commercial job, the PA will touch everything. If you want to learn about the nuts and bolts of filmmaking, commercials offer you a chance to get close to everything and feel it out. The short schedule involved in commercial shoots allows a PA to take time in between jobs to recharge and not burn out completely.

SHORT FILMS

Short films are abridged features. They have a smaller budget, a shorter schedule, and a spark that makes them incredibly fun to work on. Shorts end up being passion projects for actors and crew alike. It is a time where people get together and have fun creating something for art's sake. I had the pleasure of working as a 2nd AD on the Oscar Award–winning short *The New Tenants*. It was an incredible experience. The actors worked under ultra-low budget SAG contracts, the PAs were mostly volunteers, and the director was trying to break into the feature film world by making this his first narrative project. The atmosphere was exciting and electric.

The biggest drawback to short films is the budget. As a PA you will be asked to do a lot of tasks for little pay. Sometimes you will work for no pay at all. In this case, try to negotiate a credit or a paid gig for the producer's next project. There's always a way and these projects are too fun to walk away from.

MUSIC VIDEOS AND INDUSTRIALS

These projects are best for serious filmmakers starting out. The shoots last a few days to a week and allow a lot of hands-on experience. On my very first music video, I ended up as the assistant art director, a grip, and a cable wrangler. And that was before I knew what a PA did.

Music videos can be fun and cool creatively. The rates will vary from project to project as they do with shorts and independent features, but these types of projects are great for PAs starting out or PAs who enjoy short, flashy projects.

PA RATES & PERKS

There's a legendary Hollywood tale about the cool movie assistant who was asked to take his boss's Aston Martin to the car wash and, since he would be out anyway, drop off a script at the home of a beautiful actress. After having the car washed, the assistant drove to the home of the actress and knocked at the front door. The star herself opened the door, invited him in for a drink, then made him an offer he'd be crazy to refuse. But refuse he did, knowing he was needed back at the studio. Now that's professionalism.

The life's not really that glamorous. As PAs we are overworked and underpaid. It's the nature of the beast. The PA daily rate has not really changed in over a decade. PAs made $120 for 12 hours of work back then; they make $130 for 12 hours of work now, sometimes less. To be fair, the rate does fluctuate from job to job. Non-union jobs may pay with food, or they may toss you $100 for the day while commercials pay $200 or more for a full day with no overtime. The amount of money we make doesn't seem like much, and to be honest, if we didn't work overtime, we couldn't afford to pay the bills. But despite the meager wage, there are perks that make up the difference.

Here is a list of perks that PAs can enjoy while working staff positions on-set:

Food — Everyone loves food. The one thing that will be readily available on a film set is snacks. You don't have to steal food from Crafty to feed yourself away from work. If you wait until the end of the day and take opened perishable items home, you can feed yourself on a lower budget. Friday is the big day. This is when Crafty must throw out any food that may spoil over the weekend. Be polite and ask if you can take it home. It's better than wasting it.

Safety Rides — PAs work all hours. Sometimes it's hard to get to a location in New York City at 3:00 a.m., not to mention that it can be a little unsafe. To avoid this, PAs are offered safety rides. A safety ride is a cab ride that production will pay for, provided you follow three rules. First, you must be in the cab before a certain time in the morning and after a certain time at night; second, you cannot tip more than 15%; and third, you must pay with cash and get a receipt.

Car Rentals — If the production is far enough away and you have been hired to work on location, they may rent you a production vehicle (to be shared with the team). Production will pay for gas and tolls; they do not pick up on parking tickets. If you are working a job outside of a public transportation hub, production will pay for gas and mileage on your car to and from work.

Computer Rentals — As a Paperwork PA in this modern age, you will most likely be asked to use your personal laptop computer on-set. If this is the case, ask production for a kit rental. This amounts to $10 per day towards the use of your computer equipment. They usually cap the kit rental at $500.

Cell Phone Rental — Again, this applies more to the Paperwork PA. If you use your cell phone frequently for business, production should help cover at least part of the bill; $10 per week is typical. Crewmembers whose jobs require a great number of calls may get reimbursed at closer to $25 per week. To get paid, you must submit the top sheet of your cell phone bill with a reimbursement form.

Printer Ink — A small perk, I know, but for a Background PA this one can be useful. Due to the nature of the job, a Background PA will sometimes print the skins out at home the night before a shoot day. If you are legitimately doing this on a frequent basis, ask the office to purchase you replacement ink cartridges for your printer. More often than not, they are happy to oblige.

RESUME

Any job that you apply for will ask for a resume. Production jobs are no different. Traditionally, a resume will contain all of your previous employers' information, plus a blurb about your responsibilities with the company. A film resume will contain different information and a different structure than what you are used to seeing.

A traditional resume simply lists your jobs in chronological order with descriptions about each company, etc. Your film resume will also be in chronological order, but should be broken down further by the type of project.

There are seven categories or types of projects that you may work on during your film career. The categories include (in no particular order): feature films, television shows, independent features, commercials, short films, music videos, and industrials. To determine the category order for your personal resume, think about what types of projects you most want to work on and put those at the top. If you want a career in television, make it the first section on your resume. If you are seeking a position in a feature film, make your feature credits the top category. Once you have established the order of your categories, you must choose a layout for your resume.

STANDARD LINE FORMAT

Standard line format runs across the page. With this format you will place the category in the center of the page and list the projects that you have completed underneath in chronological order, beginning with the most recent and working backwards. Give ample spacing between jobs so that you do not clutter the page. Here is a sample of the line format:

Feature Film

Project title, date/year, producing company, 1st AD name,
2nd AD name, 2nd 2nd AD name, Your Position

Repeat this format for all of the projects that you have worked on. It contains all of the pertinent information that a film resume requires. A film resume should answer two questions:

1. What have you done?
2. Who have you worked for?

If you can answer these two questions with your resume, you're on the right track. Because of the simplicity of this format, it is great for a standard resume. If you want your resume to stand out and look a little fancier, I suggest you use a column format.

COLUMN FORMAT

The column format contains the same information as the line format. The difference is the layout of the information. I like this layout because it is more aesthetically pleasing and draws the interviewer's eye to the most important information. The column format looks like this:

Feature Film		
Project Name 1	**Project Name 2**	**Project Name 3**
Producing company	*Producing company*	*Producing company*
month/year	month/year	month/year
1st AD name	1st AD name	1st AD name
2nd AD name	2nd AD name	2nd AD name
2nd 2nd AD name	2nd 2nd AD name	2nd 2nd AD name
Your Position	**Your Position**	**Your Position**

I usually space out three columns on a letter-size piece of paper. This format breaks up the monotony of looking at line after line of information on a resume. To finish off the job section of the resume, I put a note at the bottom that simply reads: "References furnished upon request." Now that we have our job section filled out, let's move to the top of the page for the identification section.

The top of your resume should contain all of the personal information that an AD will need to get in touch with you for a job. All of this information should be centered and clearly readable.

From top to bottom provide the following information: your name, phone number, email address, and (if applicable) a website. Once all of your contact information is complete, you will be looking at a working film resume.

THE INTERVIEW

Before an AD hires a PA, he or she will usually sit the candidate down for an interview to ask questions about past experience, working style, and personality. After all of the normal formalities, what the AD is really asking you is whom have you worked with and what do they have to say about you. This is the moment where your resume comes in very handy. As a rule of thumb, always bring two or three copies of your resume to an interview. It makes you look prepared and allows you a cheat sheet when discussing your past work. The AD will take a moment to read over your resume. They pick out work details such as projects that they know of and ADs that they have worked with. Be prepared to have an opinion about your experiences. The AD wants to know what types of situations you have handled and how everything worked out. Try to walk them through your resume and allow time for them to ask questions. The AD will take the lead in the interview, but with your resume, you can guide them to see what makes you the strongest applicant.

GETTING A JOB

To get your start in the industry, think of any and all resources that you can tap. There are a few different ways to go about this.

ASK YOUR FRIENDS

First, talk to people you know; any friends or friends of friends who know someone in the industry. Express your interest in production and flat out tell them, "I'm looking for a job, do you know of any openings?" Hopefully this will get you hired right away. If, like most of us, you do not have any contacts in the industry, getting that first job will be tougher, but certainly doable.

CHECK THE WEBSITES

When I first started out I worked on a music video in Brooklyn. We shot it in a dirty warehouse with limited crew and sets. I found the job on a website called Mandy.com. Mandy is a great resource for PAs who are just starting out. While you'll find a lot of student films, you will also find calls for many independent films and shorts. The other thing to check out is the (New York City) Mayor's Office of Film, Theatre & Broadcasting. On their website you will find a list called "reel jobs." This list gives you the name of a production, the dates they are planning to shoot, and most importantly, an address. Send your resume. There are a few other websites that you can use in order to look for work, noted below from most reliable to least:

- Craigslist.org (do it once, just for the experience)
- Filmstaff.com
- Mandy.com
- Mayor's Office of Film, Theatre & Broadcasting (East Coast) *www.nyc.gov/film*
- Productionweekly.com (a paid subscription service listing information for all registered films shooting worldwide)
- TheFutonCritic.com (for a comprehensive list of projects in production or development)
- Trevanna.com
- Variety411.com (a national production directory)

COLD CALLS

Another way of finding jobs is to grab any opportunity you come across on the street. If you spot a film crew working in a neighborhood, talk to the PA on lockup. Even better, when you see a no-parking sign with a production office phone number on it, call the number. Ask if they are hiring any additional PAs. Can you send them a resume? Keep plugging away until someone says yes.

DISTINGUISH YOURSELF

To distinguish yourself from all the other PAs out there, you have to be good at what you do. Make yourself a valuable asset to the production team and they will hire you back on a regular basis. Make sure to pay attention to what is going on around you as well as what is being said on the walkie. Make sure that you don't fall in with the crowd. Learn to gauge situations and use proper judgment, but remember your place. You help to facilitate communication. You'll have to work your way up to running the show.

THE PA LADDER

You became a production assistant because you wanted to break into the film industry, but now that you're a working PA, what comes next? If you stay on the production path, you will become an Assistant Director, eventually a UPM, and finally, if you so choose, a producer or director. The PA ladder can be broken up into years. For every year that you work, you will gain invaluable experiences that will push your career to the next level. Here is the typical path a PA will follow on the way up the production ladder:

Year 1: You get your first job as an additional PA. You make a good impression on the Key PA and the ADs and get everyone's phone number so you can call them for work. Now is the time to start saving all of your call sheets and pay stubs.

Year 2: You are an experienced PA. You've spent the year assisting staff PAs on all of the additional PA jobs you've taken. You are now ready to run the game. Around this time, you will probably get your first staff job. It's time to shine.

Year 3: You've built up your reputation and moved from job to job, honing your skills, specializing, and making the connections that you will need to bump up to the next level.

Years 4, 5, & 6: If you work as much as I am lucky to do, these years will not exist. You will skip these steps and move to your main goal. If, however, you work as much as the average PA, these years will be spent perfecting the skills learned in years 1, 2, & 3.

Main Goal: Become an AD. Your mission, should you choose to accept it, is to spend your PA days learning the AD craft. In order to officially join the Directors Guild of America, a PA must complete 600 working days on a credited film set. The process takes the average PA three to six years to complete. Once you've collected all of your days, it's time to put together your AD book.

AD BOOK

Once you've been in the business this long, you will have a pretty good idea of where you would like to end up career-wise. This is the turning point. You've worked all of your required days as a PA and now have a few options. You can continue to PA and life will not really change. You can move to another department such as Camera or Props, or get out of the game altogether. If you have the stomach for the next step, you will put together your AD book and try to gain entry into the Directors Guild of America (DGA).

The first page of your AD book will be the table of contents. On this page you will fill out the title of the jobs that you have worked and the dates. The next part of your AD book is made up of three different types of paperwork. To complete it, you will need a separate DGA top sheet for each job that you've worked, call sheets or production reports for days that you worked, and pay stubs for the weeks that you worked. All paperwork in the book should be grouped together by job.

Each job constitutes one section of your AD book. The sections are organized chronologically starting with your most recent job. The first page of each section is the DGA top sheet which can be found on the DGA website *(http://www.dgaca.org/dgaca_3aql.pdf)*. Behind the top sheet you should stack your call sheets or production reports. Your name should be highlighted on all call sheets and production reports in the book. The final piece of each section is your weekly pay stubs. The simplest way to get them into your book is to make photocopies. The photocopied pay stubs will sit behind the call sheets. Once you've done this for every job on your table of contents, consider your AD book complete. It's time to turn it in.

Bring the book to your local DGA Office for approval. Once the book is approved you are eligible to go out and find work as an AD. You may work a few small jobs before you join the guild, but once you've taken a staff AD job, you must join. Your last task before entry into the guild is to collect references from ADs who will vouch for you. Start building those relationships while you are a PA.

Once your book is approved and you are a working AD, the timeline resets to year one. Consider your PA career to have been the B.C. Era; it's time to enter the year 1 AD.

AD Year 1: You are a working 2nd 2nd AD, finally getting the recognition and pay that you have earned. At this point you are jumping from job to job building up your reputation until someone offers you a shot as a Key 2nd AD.

AD Year 2: You may still be a 2nd 2nd or you may be a Key 2nd AD now. Either way, this is when you will start working more often and building up your days to be eligible for the 1st AD position.

AD Years 3, 4, & 5: These years are spent working. This is the time where you build up your contacts and learn from the 1st AD. Some ADs will stop at this point. They are happy as Key 2nd ADs and do not want the responsibility of the 1st AD position. For those who want to move on, there are years six to nine.

AD Years 6–9: Someone has given you a shot as a 1st AD. Your first assignment is to build your team. Remember all of the people that you've worked with in the past and choose the ones who work the best and work best with you. Continue to grow and make contacts in the industry as you search for an opportunity to make the leap to the next step.

AD Year 10: Hopefully before this year, but around this time, you will become a unit production manager. The UPM is also known as a line producer. Once you take this job, life is all about budgets, contracts, and approvals. I love this kind of stuff, so enjoy!

Year 50: Pat yourself on the back for surviving this long in the business and bringing entertainment to the masses. Now accept the award and get off the stage.

A quick note about this timeline; it is slightly accelerated. In the real world, there can be a lot of downtime in between projects. For example, there tends to be less work during the months of December and January because of the holidays and vacation. That's 60 PA days that you cannot count towards your book. This timeline will only hold true if you work continuously through the duration of your career. I wish you the best of luck.

FUN RESOURCES

Here is a list of websites that I've found useful to stay up to date on current news in the film and television industry.

Boxofficemojo.com – Great site for checking box office statistics and stats.

Deadlinehollywood.com – Up to the minute industry news from a business perspective brought to you by Nikki Finke.

Filmdrunk.com – Movie blog with current news about who's attached to what project and cool trailers.

Screenrant.com – TV and movie news without the sugar coating.

Warmingglow.com – A television blogg linked to Filmdrunk.

WRAPPING UP

So the last thing that I want to say to you is, thank you. There is a lot of information in this book that can be hard to comprehend and seemingly confusing. If you've stuck it out this far you may just have what it takes. You have learned about the different positions involved in production. You have also learned about the different positions involved with the working crews. While the information that I have provided is current and correct, it may not be applicable in every situation. As you work more and more you will learn to adapt your working style to the needs of your particular production. On one set you will be an additional PA, on the next you will run the background actors while working as a Paperwork PA; be ready to jump in, step up, and fill those production shoes! You now know the process of working on-set and how to fill out most of the paperwork involved in the day-to-day operations. Remember this is a hard job, but above all, have fun. The job can be a hellish nightmare or the most exciting circus around. Your attitude and the way that you work with others will determine the experience that you have. I wish you the best and look forward to working with you in the future.

Check the gate, cuz that's a wrap!

APPENDIX A

TIMING CHART

When understanding time in film, remember that we like to break everything down into its most efficient components. Time is money in the film industry. Since a dollar breaks into 10 equal parts, we divide our hours into 10 parts as well. For our purposes, this means that every tenth of an hour on your timecard (.1) is equal to 6 minutes. When calculating time for background actors or crewmembers, use this chart as a quick reference.

Minutes	Time in Decimal Form
6	0.1
12	0.2
18	0.3
24	0.4
30	0.5
36	0.6
42	0.7
48	0.8
54	0.9
60	1.0

CALCULATING MEAL PENALTIES

Meal penalties are calculated six hours after the start of the workday and six hours after the end of any official meal break. Yes, that is twice a day; once for lunch and once for dinner. In order to calculate the number of penalties, I have found a system that works simply and quickly. Note: Remember that it is the film company that is being penalized for keeping crewmembers from eating on time; for the crewmembers, it's a bonus.

1. Write down the time that the first penalty is due.

2. Write four (4) more times in 30-minute increments.

3. Between these five (5) times you've written put a dash.

4. Place the numbers 1–4 above the dashes between your times.

5. Now look at the times the crew was due for a break. If their out-times fall between any of the times you've jotted down, the number above the dash is the number of penalties owed.

6. Example: 12:00P-[1]-12:30P-[2]-1:00P-[3]-1:30P-[4]-2:00P

APPENDIX B

PREP

As discussed, one of the first things you will do when you come in for prep is build your AD kit. Here is a list of the folders and paperwork (and the number of copies) that you will need in your kit:

1. **PROJECT**
   a) Camper/Transpo Breakdown (5)
   b) Collated Scripts (4)
   c) Day Out of Days (10)
   d) Extras Breakdown (10)
   e) One-Liner (10)
   f) Script Revisions (5)
   g) Shooting Schedule (5)

2. **CREW PAPERWORK**
   a) Accident Reports (10 copies of each)
      i) Background
      ii) Cast & Crew
      iii) Loss and Damage
      iv) Vehicle

3. **ACCOUNTING**
   a) Box Kit Rental
   b) Car Allowance
   c) Cell Phone Allowance
   d) Check Request
   e) DGA Deal Memo
   f) Loanout Forms
   g) Petty Cash Envelope

h) Petty Cash Request

i) Start Work

j) Time Cards

k) W-9/I-9

4. PRODUCTION

a) Background Breakdown

b) Crew List

c) Envelopes (both letter and inter-office)

d) Exhibit G

e) Location Maps

f) Location Service Lists

g) Photo Release

h) SAG Rule Book

i) SAG and Non-SAG Vouchers

j) Vendor List

AD SUPPLY LIST

Remember, when you build your AD kit you will also be ordering supplies. On the following page you will find a list of supplies that you should include in your kit.

Production_____   Date Submitted_____

SUPPLY LIST				
Item	Description	Quantity	Cost	Total
3" binder	For your paperwork	3		
3-hole punch	For scripts and others	1		
2-hole punch	for PRs and call sheets	1		
legal/letter size clipboards	call sheet size…	3		
multi-colored pens	4-color click for PRs - fine point	3		
Bic Click Sticks - black and blue		2 boxes		
paper clips	assorted sizes, not too big	2 boxes		
binder clips	small, medium, and large sizes	2 boxes		
rubber bands	assortment	1 box		
ink for stamp	red and green Ink	2 bottles		
stamps	1 All Calls Early, 1 All Calls Later	2	Having 2 sets makes it go faster	
Sharpies	black, green, and red	2 boxes		
mechanical pencils w/ eraser		1 box		
erasable pens	black or blue	1 box		
Wite-Out tape	The small thin one that's PR-line size	2 ribbons		
Wite-Out pen		2 pens		
white 1" gaffer's tape	for labeling	1 roll		
Scotch Tape	and a small dispenser	2 rolls		
giveaway pens	something cheap	2 boxes		
calculator	nice, but not necessary	1		
production tin	opt for a side opener	1		
paper	letter size	2 reams		
paper	legal size	2 reams		
junction box	for the Internet	1-3		
printer/copier	your best friend!	hopefully 1		
copier toner	your worst enemy	2 backups		
printer ink	Switzerland… more neutral.	2 backups		
legal size football folders	for the daily paperwork	1		
legal size plastic folder	for time cards	1		
Tylenol	just in case	1 bottle		
Advil	because not everyone takes Tylenol	1 bottle		
tissues	for wiping	1 pouch		
scissors	for cutting	2		
stapler	Find one that's comfortable, you deserve it	2		
staples	to keep the stapler happy	2 boxes		
Robitussin To Go	for "those" days on set	1 box		
			Total Cost: $	

Submitted By_____   Page____ of ___   Approved By_____

Courtesy of the author.

THE PRODUCTION BINDER

While it is not necessary for you to have a production binder, making one is a good habit to get into while you're starting out. ADs will always have this binder because it contains all of the information that they will need to run an efficient shoot. Here is a breakdown of how a production binder may be put together:

- Crew list
- One-Liner
- Collated script
- Schedules
— shooting schedules
— DOOD
— continuity one-liner
- Talent
— cast deal memos
— background breakdown
- Travel memos
- Time cards for ADs & production

Besides the production binder, it is always a good idea to have a daily paperwork binder for production to examine. This book will be updated daily by the Paperwork PA. Inside this binder you will find tabs marked by numbered days of production and dates. For example: Day 1, 12/23/09. Between these tabs you will place the following paperwork in this order:

- Production report
- Camera
— purchase order
— inventory sheet
— camera reports
- Sound
— sound reports
- Script
— top summary page of notes
— copy of actual notes
— editor's log
- Exhibit G

- Background
— copy of the skins
— background breakdown sheet

This binder can be used to locate discrepancies among any paper-work you encounter while working. It makes it easy to backtrack and correct errors, because all of the information is stored chronologically in one place. It is a good idea to take the initiative to use this book. It's sure helped me.

PREP DAY 2 — INTERVIEWS

Now that all of the physical prep has been done, it's time to sit down for your interviews with Accounting and the UPM. Below you will find a list of questions that I ask on every job I get on. I start by asking the accountant and then fill in the blanks during my meeting with the UPM. I hope this helps you as much as it has me! You may not understand all of the questions or the terms on this list. Don't worry, this is my personal starting point when I work on a job. You will develop your own questions as you learn and understand how the business works.

Questions for Accounting:

1. How do you like your time cards filled out (ask because some accountants have a preference)?_____

2. What day is your weekending? _____

3. On your time card should I write in standard time (3:30) or military time (15.5)? _____

4. Should time cards reflect real time (recorded exactly down to the minute)? Or should it be broken into 6-minute increments (easily recorded as 1 hour)? _____

5. Do you take out lunch time from a PA's working hours?_____

6. Does the 1st AD receive an extended day after 14 hours of work? Does he receive a double day @ 16 hours? _____

7. Does the 2nd AD's out-time reflect 30 minutes after wrap while shooting on a stage or 1 hour after wrap while shooting on location?
_____

8. Does the 2nd AD receive a double day @ 16 hours? _____

9. Does the 2nd 2nd AD's out-time reflect last man (the last crew-member off the clock)? Or does it reflect 1 hour after wrap time?

_____

10. How do I indicate the $50 DGA wrap allowance given to an AD who stays as the last man on set the night before the company moves to a new location? _____

11. Do ADs receive meal money (a conditional $28.00 added to the AD's check)? How should I indicate it on their time card?

_____

12. Are the meal money rules as follows: ADs must be on the clock on or before 9:00 a.m. and off the clock on or after 7:30 p.m. If both of these conditions are met, the AD will receive meal money.

_____

13. What kind of comments do you want on the time cards? _____

14. Is it okay to only use the last 4 digits of an employee's social security number after filling out his initial time card?_____

15. On the time card, where do you like to start your workweek? For Ex: is the "Day 1" spot equal to Sunday? Or Monday? _____

16. How many times may production request grace in a week?_____

17. How long does a lunch grace last? 12 minutes? 15 minutes?_____

18. How do you define wrap grace? Is production entitled to ask for a 30-minute wrap grace? Or a 1-hour wrap grace?_____

19. What is the safety ride policy? What are the time constraints on taking a taxi (before 6 a.m. and after 11 p.m.)? _____ How much can a PA tip (15% or less)? _____

20. Do you prefer that we spend cash or will you issue a petty cash card? _____

21. Is Starbucks allowed and for whom?_____

22. Can a PA turn in handwritten cab receipts (receipts on the back of business cards from car services and limo companies)?_____

Notes:

_____

_____

_____

_____

You may not recognize all the words. Don't worry. This is my personal list developed through years of unique experiences. You'll quickly develop a personalized list... written on your terms. As you move from job to job you will learn what questions to ask and what applies to the situation that you are in. This list will at least get you started.

APPENDIX C

PAPERWORK

In this section you will find samples of paperwork that have been discussed in this book.

Shooting Schedule

Hooked
Shooting Schedule

"HOOKED" SHOOTING GREEN 11.21.09

Shoot Day # 1 Monday, October 26, 2009

T	CENTRAL PARK - MEADOW	DAY	**
8	Scene #: 7	Nat and Erin jump off the bridge and kiss	

st Members
1. NAT
2. ERIN
ras
  (2) EMPLOYEES
  (2) TEENS
  (6) ND PASSERBYS

Props
PIC OF MILLER'S MOM
VEGAN PIZZA
WALLET

T	PIZZA A-LA-BRUCE	DAY	**
4	Scene #: 33	Nat gets pizza, finds out where Erin works	

st Members
1. NAT
2. ERIN
ras
  (2) TEENS
  (6) ND PASSERBYS
  EMPLOYEE

Props
CELL PHONE
COMPUTER
VEGAN PIZZA

T	PIZZA A-LA-BRUCE	DAY	**
3	Scene #: 25	Nat orders pizza for Erin and himself	

st Members
1. NAT
2. ERIN
ras
  (2) TEENS
  (6) ND PASSERBYS
  EMPLOYEE

Props
PICS IN WALLET
VEGAN PIZZA
WALLET

T	CENTRAL PARK - MEADOW	DAY	**
3	Scene #: 26	Erin asks about Nat's underwear, he shows his glasses	

st Members
1. NAT
2. ERIN
ras
  (6) ND PASSERBYS

Props
GLASSES

T	BENCH ON BROADWAY	DAY	**
8	Scene #: 8	Erin and Nat eat pizza, he tells her about himself	

st Members
1. NAT
2. ERIN
ras
  (6) ND PASSERBYS

Props
VEGAN PIZZA

COMPANY MINI-MOVE

T	RANDALL'S SUPERMARKET	NIGHT	**
1	Scene #: 2	Erin shops for cat food and chocolate cake mix	

st Members
2. ERIN

Props
CAT FOOD
CELL PHONE

urtesy of the author.

One-Liner

Scheduled							

"HOOKED" SHOOTING GREEN 11.21.09

200	7	EXT	CENTRAL PARK - MEADOW Nat and Erin jump off the bridge and kiss	DAY	1 6/8	pgs.	1, 2
141	33	EXT	PIZZA A-LA-BRUCE Nat gets pizza, finds out where Erin works	DAY	1 3/8	pgs.	1, 2
100	25	EXT	PIZZA A-LA-BRUCE Nat orders pizza for Erin and himself	DAY	2/8	pgs.	1, 2
101	26	EXT	CENTRAL PARK - MEADOW Erin asks about Nat's underwear, he shows his glasses	DAY	1 7/8	pgs.	1, 2
201	8	EXT	BENCH ON BROADWAY Erin and Nat eat pizza, he tells her about himself	DAY	1 4/8	pgs.	1, 2

COMPANY MINI-MOVE

3	2	INT	RANDALL'S SUPERMARKET Erin shops for cat food and chocolate cake mix	NIGHT	4/8	pgs.	2

End Day # 1 Monday, October 26, 2009 -- Total Pages: 7 2/8

324	4	EXT	DOWNTOWN STREET Nat and Bullseye walk and talk about Erin	DAY	2	pgs.	1, 3
325	5	EXT	DOWNTOWN STREET Nat and Bullseye stop for hotdog and picture	DAY	4/8	pgs.	1, 3
327	7	EXT	DOWNTOWN STREET Nat and Bullseye watch children run to school	DAY	3/8	pgs.	1, 3

COMPANY MINI-MOVE

300	10	EXT	STORE Erin and Bullseye walk with arm loads of clothes	DAY	4/8	pgs.	2, 3
298	8	EXT	FUNERAL HOME Nat stakes out the funeral, he has to relieve himself	DAY	3/8	pgs.	1, 74A
366	10A	EXT	FUNERAL HOME Nat pees into a bottle, a van blocks him in	DAY	2/8	pgs.	1
125	17	EXT	BLOOMINGDALES Bullseye and Nat march into Bloomingdales	DAY	1/8	pgs.	1, 3
129	21	EXT	BLOOMINGDALES Bullsey tells Erin about his situation, Nat has bad news	DAY	5/8	pgs.	1, 2, 3
127	19	INT	BLOOMINGDALES Nat and Bullseye search through store for Erin	DAY	1/8	pgs.	1, 3
126	18	INT	BLOOMINGDALES Bullseye asks Tranny if she's seen Erin	DAY	2/8	pgs.	1, 3, 56
128	20	INT	BLOOMINGDALES Bullseye and Nat find Erin with a duffle of stuff	DAY	5/8	pgs.	1, 2, 3
45	3	INT	BLOOMINGDALES Bullseye spritzes the perfume girl	DAY	1 4/8	pgs.	2, 3, 27, 64
2	1	INT	BLOOMINGDALES Erin is standing at the make-up counter	DAY	6/8	pgs.	2, 21

End Day # 2 Tuesday, October 27, 2009 -- Total Pages: 8

82	7	I/E	CHURCH - NAT'S CAR Nat watches from across the street and listens	DAY	2/8	pgs.	1, 2, 3, 4, 5, 6,
83	8	EXT	CHURCH - NAT'S CAR Nat takes pictures of Erin	DAY	1/8	pgs.	1, 2, 3, 4, 5, 6,
193	A7	EXT	CHURCH Bullseye kisses Erin and they walk outside	DAY	1	pgs.	2, 3, 7

Courtesy of the author.

Day Out of Days

Mar 17, 2010
8:32 PM

Hooked
Day Out of Days Report for Cast Members

Month/Day	10/26	10/27	10/28	10/29	10/30	10/31	11/01	11/02	11/03	11/04	11/05	11/06	11/07
Day of Week	Mon	Tue	Wed	Thu	Fri	Sat	Sun	Mon	Tue	Wed	Thu	Fri	Sat
Shooting Day	1	2	3	4	5			6	7	8	9	10	
1. NAT	SW	W	W	H	W			W	W	W	W	W	
2. ERIN	SW	W	W	W	W			W	W	H	W	W	
3. BULLSEYE		SW	W	W	W			W	W	W	W	W	
4. ANNIE			SW	W	W			W	H	H	W	W	
5. BOBBY			SW	W	W			W	H	H	W	W	
6. STEVEN			SW	W	W			W	H	H	W	WD	
7. ROBERTA			SW	W	W			W	H	H	W	W	

Courtesy of the author.

Voucher

BACKGROUND VOUCHER

LEGAL LAST NAME	FIRST		SOC. SEC. NO.		WORKING HOURS			MEAL PERIODS		

CALL TIME   WEATHER   DATE

PRODUCTION/SHOW

REPORTING

SET DISMISSAL   AM   PM

PRODUCTION COMPANY

MARITAL STATUS	NO. DEP.	TAX EXEMPT?
□ SINGLE □ MARRIED		

AM FROM:
PM TO:

FROM:
TO:

NDB FROM:

MEAL PENALTIES   MEALS CATERED

Lunch   Dinner

B □   L □   D □

APPROVED FOR PAYMENT

EMPLOYEE SIGNATURE   PHONE NUMBER

X

TYPE OF	WAGES		AMOUNT	BASIC RATE
WORK	HOURS	RATE		
	WORK		WARDROBE	AMOUNT

STREET

CITY	STATE	ZIP	DAY			MEAL PEN	ADJUSTMENTS/ALLOWANCES
			1 1/2 X			MILEAGE	
			2X			ADJUSTMENT	OVERTIME

AGENCY NAME   PHONE NUMBER

PROP

STREET

AUTO

CITY	STATE	ZIP				WET/SMOKE	GROSS

YOUR EMPLOYER NAME   HAIR/MAKEUP

Courtesy of the author.

Box Kit Rental Form

BOX RENTAL WEEKLY INVOICE

PRODUCTION COMPANY: _____

EMPLOYEE: _____ S.S.#: _____

LOAN OUT COMPANY: _____

FEDERAL ID#: _____

RENTAL RATE: $ _____ PER WEEK/DAY
(Must be recorded on employee time card each week)

WEEK ENDING DATE: _____

INVENTORY: (Attach additional pages if necessary):

_____

_____

_____

_____

_____

INVENTORY: (Check one)

☐ ON FILE   ☐ ATTACHED

Employee/Loanout agree that the equipment listed herein is rented to Production Company for use under Employee/Loanout's direction and control. Employee/Loanout are solely responsible for any damage to or loss of such equipment and hereby waive any claims against _____ _____ for any loss or damage of any kind. Entertainment Partners shall have no obligation to indemnify Employee/Loanout against any losses or damage, or to provide any insurance coverage for the benefit of Employee/Loanout covering the equipment herein described. Further, the Production Company and Employee certify that the equipment listed herein is being rented at competitive rates.

I attest that the above-described equipment represents a valid rental for this production.

_____   _____
EMPLOYEE SIGNATURE   DATE

_____   _____
APPROVAL SIGNATURE   DATE

Courtesy of the author.

Petty Cash Voucher Envelope

PETTY CASH VOUCHER ENVELOPE   **Show:** _____

Employee's Name: _____   Show No. _____ Department _____

Address: _____

_____   Date: _____

Social Security No. _____

#	Date	Paid To	Description	Amount	Episode	Account
			Total			

I hereby certify that I have incurred all expenses above on behalf of the company and that they are directly related to and/or associated with the active conduct of the Company's business.

Amt. Reimbursed $ _____

Approved (Dept. Hd.) _____

Cash Received $ _____

Approved (U.P.M.) _____

By: _____

Advance Amt. $ _____

Approved (Prod. Acct.) _____

Employee Signature _____

☐ Final Settlement $ _____

NBCP - 03 R 9/04

Approved (NBCP) _____

Courtesy of the author.

Purchase Order

**PURCHASE
ORDER**

PO # / Ref:	243/2005

From (buyer):

Company Name
Address
City, State, Zip
Company Phone Number

To (seller):

Company Name
Address
City, State, Zip
Company Phone Number

Ship To Address:

Company Name
Address
City, State, Zip

Bill To Address:

Company Name
Address
City, State, Zip

Buyer contact:

Name:	John J Doe
Phone:	(678) 555-1324
Email:	John.Doe@Who.com

Date	Partial allowed?	Ship via	Shipping account number	Payment Terms
Month/Day/Year	Yes/No	Method (Air/Ground)	(If Applicable)	Deferred/Advanced/COD?

		Special Shipping Instructions:		Payment Method
				Cash/Credit/Transfer?

Item Number	Description	Quantity	Unit Price	Total Price
1023	Individual coffee packets for espresso machine	4 Boxes	$4.50	$18.00
2045	Coffee filters	2 sleeves	$2.00	$4.00

Company Details:
Company Name
Address
City, State Zip

Contact Details:
Contact Name/Title
Contact Phone #
Contact E-mail Address

SUB TOTAL	$22.00
SHIPPING CHARGES	$5.00
TAXES (If Applicable)	0.00
TOTAL	$27.00

Approved by
_____

Approved by
_____

Notes:

Courtesy of the author.

APPENDIX D

PAPERWORK SURVIVAL GUIDE

By X. Sydney Ng
Adapted by Joshua A. Friedman

- Collect any distro (distribution), mail, or packages sent down from the office, and pass it out.
- Put together your production tin in this order:
— "Yesterday" is your PR (production report)
— "Today" is your current call sheet
— "Tomorrow" is your blank PR
  - Begin getting "manpower" (finding out who's working in which department).
— Find the heads of each department and ask them these three questions:
    - "What time were you out last night?"
    - "Who is on your crew today?"
    - "Who will be on your crew tomorrow?"
  - Call the production office and tell them what time the first shot was taken. You can get this information from the Script Supervisor.
— Keep a call sheet in your pocket to jot down what time you start shooting a scene and what time you finish a scene.
  - Once you have finished getting all of the manpower, give your list to the 2nd AD to put onto the back of the call sheet.
  - You may have to call the Locations Department to get information on the nearest hospital and the holding space (gathering area for extras) if you are going to be on location the following day.
  - Next, get the weather report for the following day.
— Include sunrise and sunset times.

— You may have to call the production office if there is no Internet connection.

• On location, the call sheet may have to be faxed to the production office. Be prepared to look for a fax machine; the Locations Department can help.

• Remember to call the office and tell them every first and last shot in a scene. Be specific and tell them if there is a change in the shooting order.

• Remember to continue passing out distro as it arrives.

• When the prelim is ready, proofread it and make copies for department heads and their seconds.

— The prelim should be printed on different colored paper to avoid confusion with a call sheet.

• Scout the location for restaurants and keep a stock of menus.

— If there is a walk away lunch, you will order for the director and producers. Have menus and options handy.

— These places must take credit cards (depending on the production).

• Call the office and tell them you've broken for lunch the minute the AD calls it out.

• Call the office right after lunch (depending on production protocol) and give them the lunch break report from the Script Supervisor.

— Stand by to get the first shot after lunch. too.

• Prep the production report throughout the day.

— Copy call sheet info for scene orders.

— Write in first and last shots as they happen.

— Copy manpower onto the back.

• Prep time cards for the production staff to make your night easier on Friday.

• Use the double-sided feature on your printer so that you use only one sheet of paper to copy both sides of the call sheet. Some people have actually used two sheets of paper to copy a call sheet and killed three baby trees.

— Staple any directions or attachments.

— Check with the UPM about the order, but traditionally a memo goes on top of the call sheet and the directions always go under a call sheet.
  • Make sure to give the Transportation Department call sheets and directions to all locations.
  • Give the 1st Team PA call sheets.
— Have enough for Hair, Makeup, Wardrobe, actors, and actors' assistants.
  • Save some call sheets for the next day and turn the rest over to the Key PA.
  • Make sure that the AD kit is well-stocked with the proper paperwork.
  • At the end of the day, get the official wrap time from Scripty.
— Get out-times for all departments.
  • If you are on location, give the crew a heads up when the honeywagon is about to leave or when the last bathrooms will be closing up.
  • At the end of the night you must collect the following for the PR.
— Camera reports
— Exhibit G
— Background breakdown
— Sound reports
— Script notes
— Original call sheet for the next day
— Wardrobe out-times
— Catering receipt (pink copy) with proper head count for crew meals
— Any startwork, incident/accident reports, or time cards
  • If ANY accidents occur you MUST call the production office immediately and inform the UPM.
— Fill out the necessary paperwork and be as detailed as possible when explaining the situation to the office.
  • Make copies of the production report.
— 5 copies go in an envelope for ADs, producers, and the Camera Department.
— You keep two copies for your record.
  • Make two copies of the script notes.

— One copy gets turned in to the office.

— One copy and the original script notes go back to the Script Supervisor.

      ■ Put Scripty's notes in the to-set box for the following day.

   • Hand in a "Red Line" PR.

— Production report, neatly corrected in red ink if any changes from the night before need to be indicated.

Once all of this is done, the Paperwork PA still has to fill out all of the time card information for ADs and the PAs. On Fridays, they assemble all of the production reports from the week and pass "cheat sheets" out to all department heads. Give them out quickly and you'll have your time cards back faster at the end of the night.

APPENDIX E

UNIONS

Labor in the film industry is represented by unions. PAs are non-union labor. We do not have a collective bargaining agreement or a health insurance plan. Once you've paid your dues, you may decide to move away from the production track. Here are some tidbits about the unions that you may choose to join. If you want to know more, check their websites and read over the union contracts.

DGA — Directors Guild of America
- Established in 1936 by a small group of directors
- Currently boasts over 14,000 members
- Membership comprises directors, ADs, UPMs, and stage managers
- Their website is *www.DGA.org*

Teamsters (IBT) — International Brotherhood of Teamsters
- Established as a Brotherhood in 1903
- Current membership is 1.4 million
- Theatrical membership includes drivers, loaders, and laborers
- The union consists of 21 divisions specializing in different types of labor
- Their website is *www.Teamster.org*

WGA — Writers Guild of America
- Revived in its current incarnation in 1933
- Membership is made up of screenwriters
- The union will register scripts
- Their website is *www.WGA.org*

SAG — Screen Actors Guild
- Established in 1933 as a way of fighting the studios for artists' rights
- SAG has jurisdiction in film, television, and commercials
- Membership of 120,000
- Membership includes actors, singers, dancers, and special talent
- Their website is *www.SAG.org*

AFTRA — American Federation of Television and Radio Artists
- Founded in 1952 in a merger of unions representing radio and television artists
- AFTRA has jurisdiction in TV, soap operas, cable, radio, music videos, commercials, games, and the Internet
- AFTRA does not have jurisdiction in motion pictures
- Membership is over 70,000
- Will sometimes ally with SAG in negotiations
- Their website is *www.AFTRA.org*

IATSE — International Alliance of Theatrical Stage Employees
- Established in 1886 with Local 1
- Currently has over 110,000 members
- Membership includes workers in the camera, sound, grip, electric, props, scenic, and set dressing departments
- Their website is *www.IATSE-INTL.org*

APPENDIX F

UNION CONTRACTS & PAPERWORK

You can find:

Commercial contracts at:
http://www.sag.org/content/commercial-contracts

Feature film contracts at:
http://www.sag.org/content/theatrical-film-contracts

Television contracts at:
http://www.sag.org/content/television-contracts

APPENDIX G

GLOSSARY OF TERMS

A

Abby: The second-to-last shot of the day.

Above-the-Line: Any production member who is salaried. Usually this includes the producers, the director, and sometimes the Director of Photography.

Actors: People who perform in front of the camera while it is filming.

Adjustment: An increase in pay for actors. An adjustment is applied to their basic rate (not to be confused with a bump).

Assistant Director: A member of the Production Department who facilitates the day-to-day running of a set.

Assistant Locations Manager: Helps the Locations Manager and works as a locations contact on-set.

Assistant Property Master: Facilitates and organizes the use of props on-set.

B

Background Actors: Actors without lines who work behind the principal actors.

Background Breakdown: A summary sheet with all of the background information from the current day.

Background Check-In: The process of signing in background, taking attendance.

Background PA: The production assistant in charge of the background actors.

Below-the-Line: Any production member who is paid on an hourly basis. This includes all working crews and labor.

Best Boy: Facilitates the gaffer's requests to the rest of the Electric crew.

BK/McDonald's Headset: A walkie-talkie headset with a protruding microphone similar to those seen at a fast food restaurant.

Boom Operator: Holds the boom mike to record.

Boom: A long pole with a microphone at the end.

Brick Box: Box used to store and separate hot and cold bricks.

Brick: A walkie-talkie battery. Can either be hot (charged) or cold (dead).

Bump: A fixed amount of money added to an employee's paycheck.

C

Call Sheet: It has every piece of information you'll need to know for the shooting day.

Camera Frame: The space being seen by the "eye" of the camera.

Camera Operator: Physically moves the camera in a shot to keep the director's vision within the proper frame.

Camera PA: The Production Assistant who assists the Camera Department.

Camera Report: A form that contains information about magazines for film, film inventory, and processing instructions. Turned in on a nightly basis with the film.

Cans: A headset attached to a receiver that clips to a belt. Used to listen to actors being recorded while filming.

Cast Chair: A wooden chair with a fabric seat and back, also known as a director's chair.

Catch: When an actor is sent to set without being accompanied by a member of production, a PA will greet or "catch" that actor when he arrives at his destination.

Catered Lunch: Lunch served by a catering service (includes breakfast in the cost).

Check the Gate: Checking the camera aperture for dust specs and hair that could ruin the image on the exposed film.

Counting the Line: Process of counting the number of cast and crewmembers who eat at catering.

Craft Service: The food service employees on-set. Often called "Crafty."

Crew Call: The time that the crew should report to work.

C-Stand: Three-legged stand with extendable arms used to hold grip equipment.

D

Dailies: Tapes or DVDs of the scenes shot over the previous days.

Day Players: Actors who work on-set for only a few days at a time. They are on daily or weekly SAG contracts.

DGA Trainee: A PA who is attached to the Directors Guild Program.

Diffusions: Fabric placed in front of lights to soften the intensity.

Director of Photography: Responsible for the mood and look of the lighting. Also known as "cinematographer."

Director: The person who controls the creative look of the project.

Distro: Paperwork sent from the office to be distributed on-set.

Dolly Grip: The member of the Grip Department who pushes the dolly.

Dolly: A cart used to move the camera, usually set on a track.

E

Electric Department: Responsible for providing all power to the set. Technicians are called electricians or "electrics."

Exhibit G: A summary of the actors' schedule recorded by a 1st Team PA.

Extras: Actors in a scene who do not have any on-camera dialogue.

F

Featured Extra: Extra who has no spoken lines in a scene but who plays a specific role.

Fire Watch: A type of lockup where a PA will guard equipment while others are away.

First (1st) AD : The person who runs the day-to-day operation on the set.

First (1st) Assistant Cameraman: Adjusts the zoom and focus of the camera. The operator's right-hand man.

First (1st) Team PA: In charge of coordinating the logistics of preparing first team for their workday.

First (1st) Team Rehearsal: Rehearsal with the main actors.

First Team: Any principal cast member is considered part of First Team.

Flag: A square frame with fabric folded over it used by grips to bend and shape light.

Frame Lines: The borders of the camera frame.

Frame Up: Move the camera to focus on a certain point.

G

Gaff: A stick used to flick lights on and off.

Gaffer: Directs the setup of lights on-set.

Gels: Filters that change the color, temperature, or intensity of light.

Genny Operator: In charge of operating and maintaining the power generator.

Going through the Works: Process of getting an actor through Hair, Makeup, and Wardrobe.

Grip: A crewmember who sets up track, helps shape light, and assists in miscellaneous construction jobs on-set.

H

Hair: The department that styles and adjusts hair.

Hand Mike: A speaker/microphone combo commonly use by truckers that fits in the palm of the hand. It is used mostly by locations, grips, and electrics.

Handheld: A camera mode in which the camera is carried by the operator without a rig attached.

Hard Lock: A lockup in which no one gets through.

Hi-Boy: A retractable stand used to hold lights and flags.

Holding: A room in which to gather background actors.

Honeywagon: The truck that contains bathrooms, dressing rooms, and a production office.

I

Industrials: Educational tapes, training videos, and business presentations.

In-Times: The time that a crewmember starts to work.

K

Keeping Eyes: Watching for a person who has wandered away from set. If an actor walks to Crafty, you may follow them over and "keep eyes" on them.

Key Grip: Head of the Grip Department.

Key Hairstylist: Head of the Hair Department.

Key Makeup Artist: Head of the Makeup Department.

Key PA: Head of the production assistants.

L

Lamp Operator: An Electric in charge of setting up the lights and running power to the set.

Last Looks: The last chance for the Hair, Makeup, and Wardrobe departments to touch up an actor before shooting.

Lavaliere: A wireless sound transmitter and a long wired microphone that can be hidden under an actor's clothing ("lav" for short).

Letting It Live: Keeping a safe lockup, but letting passersby walk through the scene as long as they don't stop in front of the camera.

Light Meter: A tool used to measure the amount of light hitting an object.

Loader: In charge of loading the camera magazines and switching out film stocks.

Load-In: The process of moving equipment into a location.

Load-Out: The process of moving equipment out of a location.

Locations Coordinator: Plans and coordinates the use of locations before the shooting crew arrives.

Locations Manager: In charge of coordinating each location that is used on a shooting day.

Locations PA: Production assistants who work with the Locations Department.

Lockup: Stopping people from entering the camera shot. A PA's bread and butter.

Lookie Loos: Anyone who is not part of the film crew, but stops (usually in the camera frame) to watch the show.

Low-Boy: A retractable stand used to hold lights and flags.

M

Mag: Short for magazine, a cartridge that contains film.

Makeup: The department that deals with facial makeup, body scars, tattoos, etc.

Manpower: A list of crewmembers working on a particular day.

Marker: A camera crewmember who lays down different colors of tape on the floor to mark where each actor stands.

Marking Rehearsal: A rehearsal with the principal actors to establish their positions.

Martini: The last shot of the night.

Meal Penalty: Money paid to actors, background, and crewmembers if they do not get a scheduled break on time.

N

Night Premium: 10% of actors' base rates-per-hour added to their paycheck.

Non-Deductible Breakfast: A 15-minute break that is not deducted from work time. Used by production to avoid meal penalties it would otherwise have to pay.

Non-SAG Actors: Actors with no union affiliation.

O

Oner: A scene that is completed in one setup. Pronounced "won-er."

On-Set Dresser: A set dresser who works with the shooting crew.

Out-Time: The time when employees go off the clock.

P

Pan Left: Swivel the camera to the left.

Paperwork PA: A production assistant in charge of summarizing and gathering all information about the shooting day.

Photo Double: A background actor filmed in place of a principal actor's body.

Photo Shoot: A project involving photos instead of film.

Picture Car: Any car used on-camera.

Principal Actor: The stars of the project.

Process Trailer: A rig used to haul a car, cameras, and some crew.

Producer: The overseer of the project who brings together the crew and the concept.

Production Assistant: An entry-level job with a lot of potential.

Production Managers: In charge of keeping the project on schedule and under budget.

Production Report: A summary of all the information about the present shooting day.

Prop Assistant: Assistant to the Property Master.

Prop Shopper: The person who buys the props and stocks whatever is needed.

Property Master: The head of the Prop Department.

Propping Up: Process of supplying actors (both principals and extras) with props.

Props: An object that can be held and carried by an actor.

Pursuit Car: Car with a long crane arm and a camera attached. Used for fast moving car chases.

R

Raking Shot: A moving camera shot in which the camera slides horizontally across an axis.

Red Line PR: An updated production report with all changes noted in red ink.

Rolling: The camera is rolling film and recording the action.

Roll Tracking: Recording the name and number of rolls (both film and sound) used during a shooting day.

S

SAG Actor: An actor affiliated with the Screen Actors Guild.

Scenic: An on-set artist responsible for any artistic jobs involving painting or crafts.

Script Supervisor: Responsible for continuity from scene to scene.

Second (2nd) AD: In charge of preparing the next day's work.

Second (2nd) Assistant Cameraman: Responsible for setting marks and keeping track of shots and takes.

Second Second (2nd 2nd) AD: Sets extras and checks all paperwork.

Second Team Rehearsal: A rehearsal with the stand-ins.

Second Unit: A separate film crew that works concurrently with the main unit. This is used to shoot scenes that do not involve principal actors.

Set Costumers: Wardrobe artists who dress the actors.

Set Dresser: Moves furniture and adjusts pieces of the set to the director's wishes.

Setting Background: The process of positioning extras into a scene.

Sound Reports: A form that contains information about sound rolls, different takes, and which microphone the sound was recorded on. Turned in on a nightly basis with the sound disc.

Staging: A safe place to keep equipment, crew, and lookie loos out of the frame of the camera.

Stars: The main actors in a film. Numbers 1 and 2 on the call sheet.

Stunt Coordinator: In charge of choreographing and ensuring the safety of all stunts performed in a production.

Stunt Players: Stuntmen/women who work in place of principal actors for dangerous scenes.

Shop Steward: Local representative of the International Alliance of Theatrical Stage Employees (IATSE)

Short End: Unexposed film left over from an exposed roll of film. Short ends are stored for use on inserts or cutaways so that film is not wasted.

Sides: Small copies of all of the script pages to be shot that day.

Skins: A list of the background actors' names and what part they play in each scene.

Slate Name: The name of the shot written on the clapboard.

Slate: Clapboard with all of the information used to identify a scene.

Sound Mixer: Controls the input and recording of sound on a mix cart.

Special Ability: An actor with a special talent.

Stand-In: An extra who substitutes for a principal actor while the crew sets up the shot.

Star Trailer: A large camper with a bedroom, living room, dining room, and mini-kitchen.

Steadicam: A camera rig that smoothes and stabilizes the movements of the camera mounted on it.

Surveillance Headset: A wraparound earpiece with a separate microphone that is conveniently worn on the head.

T

TCD: The Traffic Control Department helps secure streets for the film crew.

TCD Officers: Officers who assist film sets in blocking and coordinating traffic flows.

Teamster: Crewman of the Transportation Department who is a member of the International Brotherhood of Teamsters. See Appendix E.

Three-Banger: A trailer with three rooms.

Traffic Lockup: A lockup that involves stopping cars with the help of the Traffic Control Department.

Transpo: Nickname for the Transportation Department.

Transportation Captain: Coordinates all vans, trucks, and transportation needs.

Two-Banger: A trailer with two rooms.

Two-Shot: A shot that frames two actors.

U

Unit Production Manager: The head of the below-the-line (paid hourly) employees. The unit production manger (UPM) is the production supervisor on-set. She approves all budgets and schedules, signs the checks, and ensures that production stays on schedule.

Utility Sound Tech: Keeps track of and monitors the sound tracks recorded with each take, and documents the appropriate paperwork.

V

Video Village: Where the producers and director sit to watch each shot.

Voucher: Paperwork for the background actors.

W

Walk and Talk: A scene in which a moving camera tracks two (or more) actors holding a conversation while walking.

Walk Away Lunch: A lunch where the crew steps away to eat on their own.

Walkie PA: The production assistant in charge of walkie-talkies and batteries.

Wardrobe: Any article of clothing worn on camera.

Wardrobe Change: A change of outfits in between scenes. Used to distinguish different days within the time period of a film.

Wardrobe Supervisor: Coordinates, maintains, and sets up all costumes for the actors on set (or in a dressing room). Delegates between one or two assistants.

Wild Tracks: Sound with no accompanying image, used to turn background sounds into white noise.

Wire: Slang term for a wireless microphone.

Wireless Microphone: A wireless transmitter pack that is hidden on an actor's person while a wire is run under the actor's clothing to capture the sound.

Z

Zone: The distance at which the crew and/or background actors get paid for their travel time.

ABOUT THE AUTHOR

© *Mark Romanelli 2010*

Joshua A. Friedman is a working production assistant in New York City. Born in Stamford, Connecticut, he moved to the state of Georgia at the age of twelve. There he became interested in theater and film, working on many productions and documentaries before studying theater at the University of Maryland. After graduating in 2005, he moved to New York City where he currently resides. Over the past three years, Mr. Friedman has worked on *Law & Order: Criminal Intent, Fringe, Gossip Girl, Royal Pains, Kings,* and *30 Rock,* as well as many feature films, including *Hancock, The Taking of Pelham 123, Salt, The Adjustment Bureau, The Beaver, It's Kind of a Funny Story, The Oranges*, and *My Idiot Brother.* He recently completed work as a 2nd AD on the Oscar-winning short film *The New Tenants.*

If you have any questions or comments you can reach Mr. Friedman at Ultimate.PA.Guide@gmail.com.

FILM PRODUCTION MANAGEMENT
2ND EDITION
MANAGEMENT AND COORDINATION IN A DIGITAL AGE

DEBORAH S. PATZ

Known as "the Swiss Army knife of production management," *Film Production Management 101* is actually two books in one — the essential open-on-the-desk guide for both production managers and coordinators. Patz takes you on a journey from development and pre-visualization to postproduction and audit, covering everything with detailed insights, humorous production stories and the inside scoop on working in film and television production.

Film Production Management 101 and Patz' previous *Surviving Production* were quickly adopted as "the" essential road map to the business and logistics of on-the-job film & television production since 1997. Originally developed from practical tools Patz created for her film and television production career, this new edition has undergone a comprehensive update to address the shifting balance between digital and film technologies and to pave the way as we progress further into the digital age. The book includes everything from budgeting, to managing the production office, to script revisions, to cost reporting, to copyright, to publicity, and much, much more. With Patz' penchant for sharing knowledge and her knack for communicating concepts, *Film Production Management 101* continues to be the book you have to have open on your desk for every prep, shoot, and wrap day. The more than 50 useful forms and checklists which are included (and downloadable) will save you time, money, and headaches, working like a pro right from day one.

"At last the complex relationship between the creation of a film and the day-to-day production management and coordination of that film is spelled out in clear, readable, and accurate detail. Deborah has written a wonderful book which should be extremely helpful to novice low-budget independent filmmakers and seasoned professionals alike."

> — Sharon McGowan, Independent Producer and Assistant Professor
> University of British Columbia Film Program

"An invaluable and comprehensive guide. Deborah Patz has drawn on her own experience and has written a thoroughly researched and helpful book."

> — Norman Jewison, Producer/Director, *The Hurricane, Moonstruck, Fiddler on the Roof*

DEBORAH PATZ has been a filmmaker on award-winning productions since the mid-1980s, primarily as a production manager and coordinator, and then as production executive. She has worked with Lucasfilm, IMAX, MCA/Universal, Alliance/Atlantis, Nelvana, BBC, CBC, the Disney Channel, and the list goes on.

$39.95 · 500 PAGES · ORDER NUMBER 147RLS · ISBN: 9781932907773

FILM & VIDEO BUDGETS
5TH EDITION

DEKE SIMON

BEST SELLER
OVER 45,000 COPIES SOLD!

Film & Video Budgets 5th Edition is a budget-making toolkit. Whether you're making a feature, a short, a documentary, an industrial or corporate, a music video, or a student film, you'll find sample budgets, complete explanations for budget line items, and tons of useful background information on High-Definition workflow updated for the 5th edition that will apply to every project you do. Plus, purchasing the book grants you access to the MWP website, where you can download all the budget templates for free. Adapt these for your own use, saving yourself hundreds of hours of tedious data entry.

For over a decade, this classic budgeting book has helped filmmakers figure out:
  · How do I put a budget together?
  · How much will my project will cost?
  · How do I build an impressive-looking budget
    for investors and funders?
... and answers to hundreds of questions you may not even have thought of yet!

The 5th edition of this all-time standard includes NEW material on preproduction and High-Definition, as well as an update of all budgets.

"Wow, just when you think you know everything about developing and producing a film, along comes another edition of Film and Video Budgets *to make you even smarter. I love those Desperate Measures sections, too."*

— Mary J. Schirmer, screenwriter, instructor
www.screenplayers.net

"The information here is truly invaluable for starting film producers. Easy to read, this gives you what you need to know to better budget your film. The new edition provides up-to-date info, so that whether you're making anything from shorts to features, you'll be well prepared."

— Erin Corrado, *www.onemoviefiveviews.com*

DEKE SIMON is a writer/producer/director of documentary, dramatic, and informational programs for television and education. His work has been honored with numerous awards, including two L.A. Emmy Awards, and four L.A. Emmy nominations.

$29.95 · 477 PAGES · ORDER NUMBER 143RLS · ISBN: 9781932907735

MAKING IT BIG IN SHORTS
2ND EDITION
THE ULTIMATE FILMMAKER'S GUIDE TO SHORT FILMS

KIM ADELMAN

Grab a camera, make a short film. Show it at Sundance; show it on YouTube. There's no limit to what you can achieve by starting small and dreaming big.

In easy-to-follow steps, short-film guru, Kim Adelman, shows you how to achieve your dreams by making that killer short film. Bringing together the artistic and business sides of filmmaking, this book gives filmmakers the skills to develop unique shorts that are creatively satisfying and can launch careers.

This Second Edition of the best-selling *The Ultimate Filmmaker's Guide to Short Films* addresses new avenues for short filmmakers, including 48-hour filmmaking challenges, and new media opportunities such as YouTube, iTunes, and the iPhone.

If you want to make it big in short films, this is the book you need.

"Kim is the undisputed queen of the short-film world. No one has a better resume, better relationships, and more passion for this particular art form than she does, and her willingness to share this knowledge, especially the hard-won lessons, is inspiring."
— Mark Stolaroff, Producer/Founder, No Budget Film School

"An essential guide for anybody who wants to make short films, which is great, because I love the short-film format. It's the best!"
— Bill Plympton, Oscar-nominated Animator: *Guard Dog, I Married a Strange Person, www.plymptoons.com*

"A practical, down-to-earth, soup-to-nuts manual on getting the most out of the short-film experience — from succinct tips on all phases of production, to making the most out of the film festival experience, and beyond. A must-read for any filmmaker who values thorough advice delivered with energy, humor, and a sincere affection for the medium."
— Christian Gaines, Director of Festivals, Withoutabox – a division of IMDb.com

Kim Adelman produced 19 short films that played at over 150 film festivals, worldwide, and won 30+ awards. She currently is the short-film correspondent for the acclaimed independent film news service indieWIRE. Additionally, Adelman teaches "Making and Marketing the Short Film" and "Low Budget Filmmaking" at UCLA Extension, and leads filmmaking workshops across the United States, Canada, and New Zealand.

$22.95 · 264 PAGES · ORDER NUMBER 128RLS · ISBN: 9781932907582

FILMMAKING FOR TEENS
2ND EDITION
PULLING OFF YOUR SHORTS

TROY LANIER & CLAY NICHOLS

BEST SELLER

With over 20 hours of video being uploaded to YouTube every minute, how can a young filmmaker possibly stand out? By reading and applying the tools of *Filmmaking for Teens* young filmmakers can learn everything they need to know about how to make a great short film.

The updated edition of this classic manual for young filmmakers includes numerous additions reflecting the enormous changes impacting the world of digital video.

New and up-to-date information on:
- shooting in HD
- advances in digital audio recording equipment
- editing and compressing video for online delivery
- maximizing your exposure on video sharing sites like YouTube
- marketing and audience development strategies for online video
- how to make money from the online video revolution

"Filmmaking for Teens is an excellent textbook geared to the young reader but with sage advice that most professionals follow. The book is comprehensive yet simple and easily comprehended. Film production is not a simple task, but reading this text makes it approachable for the high school student. It demystifies a complicated field."

> — Jane Jackson, Assistant Chair of the Communication Department,
>   State University of New York

"Filmmaking for Teens, 2nd Ed. makes for an easy read with loads of information in a concise way. This book will give you the edge you need to get a jump-start into the world of film. A perfect book for starting filmmakers."

> — Erin Corrado, www.onemoviefiveviews.com

TROY LANIER and CLAY NICHOLS have gone on to become pioneers in the online video industry. Producers of the acclaimed series *DadLabs*, the pair has produced over 500 episodes of web TV that have garnered millions of viewers. They will be using this platform to promote *Filmmaking for Teens*, 2nd edition to parents and kids alike though the creation of a series of web videos, shared on both the extensive DadLabs distribution network, and on a dedicated YouTube channel. The masters of online video practice exactly what they preach based on the principles of this book.

$26.95 · 240 PAGES · ORDER NUMBER 132RLS · ISBN 13: 9781932907643

DIGITAL VIDEO SECRETS
WHAT THE PROS KNOW AND
THE MANUALS DON'T TELL YOU

TONY LEVELLE

It's a fact that manufacturers use the same chips in their low-end cameras as their expensive cameras. A few simple tricks will make your camera deliver professional quality images. Sony, Panasonic, and Canon won't tell you that – but Levelle will.

Here are 100 simple digital video shooting secrets that "everyone knows" but no one will tell you. This is a "cheat sheet book" for every first-time filmmaker which is filled with practical ready-to-use information.

As the resolution of digital video cameras increases and their price decreases, the line between professional and consumer features is blurring. Get the most from your camera and start producing professional quality images.

"Very clear and precise. A layman can take this book and eliminate massive amounts of mistakes and actually make good movies."
> – Alan Siegel, California Teacher of the Year (2005),
> teacher at nationally recognized, award-winning Carle High School

"Tony Levelle has put between two covers everything you need to know about the best and brightest ways to use your digital camera, regardless of what you're shooting – from wedding videos to the next big ground-breaking low-budget sensation."
> – John Gaspard, Author, *Digital Filmmaking 101, Fast, Cheap & Under Control* and *Fast, Cheap & Written That Way*

"Digital Video Secrets is not only a terrific introduction to the craft of visual language, it offers up many of the purest essentials that experienced filmmakers often neglect. Tony Levelle has, quite simply, assembled a wonderfully proficient guidebook."
> – Richard D. Pepperman, Author, *Film School, The Eye Is Quicker*, and *Setting Up Your Scenes*

"Clear and concise, with hard-earned experiences interspersed throughout, this book will help you learn the rules of filmmaking and then how to break them. Filmmakers should keep this one in their back pocket as a reference."
> – Devin Watson, Producer, *The Cursed*

Besides writing hundreds of corporate instructional manuals and making dozens of videos, TONY LEVELLE recently co-authored *Producing with Passion: Making Films That Change the World.*

$24.95 · 200 PAGES · ORDER NUMBER 88RLS · ISBN 13: 9781932907476

24 HOURS | **1.800.833.5738** | WWW.MWP.COM

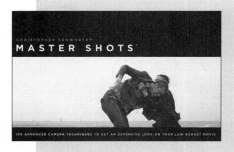

MASTER SHOTS
100 ADVANCED CAMERA TECHNIQUES TO GET AN
EXPENSIVE LOOK ON YOUR LOW BUDGET MOVIE

CHRISTOPHER KENWORTHY

Master Shots gives filmmakers the techniques they need to execute complex, original shots on any budget. By using powerful master shots and well-executed moves, directors can develop a strong style and stand out from the crowd. Most low-budget movies look low-budget, because the director is forced to compromise at the last minute. *Master Shots* gives you so many powerful techniques that you'll be able to respond, even under pressure, and create knock-out shots. Even when the clock is ticking and the light is fading, the techniques in this book can rescue your film, and make every shot look like it cost a fortune.

Each technique is illustrated with samples from great feature films and computer-generated diagrams for absolute clarity.

Use the secrets of the master directors to give your film the look and feel of a multi-million-dollar movie. The set-ups, moves and methods of the greats are there for the taking, whatever your budget.

"Master Shots gives every filmmaker out there the blow-by-blow setup required to pull off even the most difficult of setups found from indies to the big Hollywood blockbusters. It's like getting all of the magician's tricks in one book."
— Devin Watson, Producer, *The Cursed*

"Though one needs to choose any addition to a film book library carefully, what with the current plethora of volumes on cinema, Master Shots *is an essential addition to any worthwhile collection."*
— Scott Essman, Publisher, *Directed By* Magazine

"Christopher Kenworthy's book gives you a basic, no holds barred, no shot forgotten look at how films are made from the camera point of view. For anyone with a desire to understand how film is constructed — this book is for you."
— Matthew Terry, Screenwriter/Director, Columnist
www.hollywoodlitsales.com

Since 2000, CHRISTOPHER KENWORTHY has written, produced, and directed drama and comedy programs, along with many hours of commercial video, tv pilots, music videos, experimental projects, and short films. He's also produced and directed over 300 visual FX shots. In 2006 he directed the web-based Australian UFO Wave, which attracted many millions of viewers. Upcoming films for Kenworthy include *The Sickness* (2009) and *Glimpse* (2011).

$24.95 · 240 PAGES · ORDER NUMBER 91RLS · ISBN: 9781932907513

 # THE MYTH OF MWP

In a dark time, a light bringer came along, leading the curious and the frustrated to clarity and empowerment. It took the well-guarded secrets out of the hands of the few and made them available to all. It spread a spirit of openness and creative freedom, and built a storehouse of knowledge dedicated to the betterment of the arts.

The essence of the Michael Wiese Productions (MWP) is empowering people who have the burning desire to express themselves creatively. We help them realize their dreams by putting the tools in their hands. We demystify the sometimes secretive worlds of screenwriting, directing, acting, producing, film financing, and other media crafts.

By doing so, we hope to bring forth a realization of 'conscious media' which we define as being positively charged, emphasizing hope and affirming positive values like trust, cooperation, self-empowerment, freedom, and love. Grounded in the deep roots of myth, it aims to be healing both for those who make the art and those who encounter it. It hopes to be transformative for people, opening doors to new possibilities and pulling back veils to reveal hidden worlds.

MWP has built a storehouse of knowledge unequaled in the world, for no other publisher has so many titles on the media arts. Please visit www.mwp.com where you will find many free resources and a 25% discount on our books. Sign up and become part of the wider creative community!

Onward and upward,

Michael Wiese
Publisher/Filmmaker

FILM & VIDEO BOOKS

TO RECEIVE A FREE MWP NEWSLETTER, CLICK ON WWW.MWP.COM TO REGISTER

SCREENWRITING | WRITING

And the Best Screenplay Goes to... | Dr. Linda Seger | $26.95
Archetypes for Writers | Jennifer Van Bergen | $22.95
Bali Brothers | Lacy Waltzman, Matthew Bishop, Michael Wiese | $12.95
Cinematic Storytelling | Jennifer Van Sijll | $24.95
Could It Be a Movie? | Christina Hamlett | $26.95
Creating Characters | Marisa D'Vari | $26.95
Crime Writer's Reference Guide, The | Martin Roth | $20.95
Deep Cinema | Mary Trainor-Brigham | $19.95
Elephant Bucks | Sheldon Bull | $24.95
Fast, Cheap & Written That Way | John Gaspard | $26.95
Hollywood Standard – 2nd Edition, The | Christopher Riley | $18.95
Horror Screenwriting | Devin Watson | $24.95
I Could've Written a Better Movie than That! | Derek Rydall | $26.95
Inner Drives | Pamela Jaye Smith | $26.95
Moral Premise, The | Stanley D. Williams, Ph.D. | $24.95
Myth and the Movies | Stuart Voytilla | $26.95
Power of the Dark Side, The | Pamela Jaye Smith | $22.95
Psychology for Screenwriters | William Indick, Ph.D. | $26.95
Reflections of the Shadow | Jeffrey Hirschberg | $26.95
Rewrite | Paul Chitlik | $16.95
Romancing the A-List | Christopher Keane | $18.95
Save the Cat! | Blake Snyder | $19.95
Save the Cat! Goes to the Movies | Blake Snyder | $24.95
Screenwriting 101 | Neill D. Hicks | $16.95
Screenwriting for Teens | Christina Hamlett | $18.95
Script-Selling Game, The | Kathie Fong Yoneda | $16.95
Stealing Fire From the Gods, 2nd Edition | James Bonnet | $26.95
Talk the Talk | Penny Penniston | $24.95
Way of Story, The | Catherine Ann Jones | $22.95
What Are You Laughing At? | Brad Schreiber | $19.95
Writer's Journey – 3rd Edition, The | Christopher Vogler | $26.95
Writer's Partner, The | Martin Roth | $24.95
Writing the Action Adventure Film | Neill D. Hicks | $14.95
Writing the Comedy Film | Stuart Voytilla & Scott Petri | $14.95
Writing the Killer Treatment | Michael Halperin | $14.95
Writing the Second Act | Michael Halperin | $19.95
Writing the Thriller Film | Neill D. Hicks | $14.95
Writing the TV Drama Series, 2nd Edition | Pamela Douglas | $26.95
Your Screenplay Sucks! | William M. Akers | $19.95

FILMMAKING

Film School | Richard D. Pepperman | $24.95
Power of Film, The | Howard Suber | $27.95

PITCHING

Perfect Pitch – 2nd Edition, The | Ken Rotcop | $19.95
Selling Your Story in 60 Seconds | Michael Hauge | $12.95

SHORTS

Filmmaking for Teens, 2nd Edition | Troy Lanier & Clay Nichols | $24.95
Making It Big in Shorts | Kim Adelman | $22.95

BUDGET | PRODUCTION MANAGEMENT

Film & Video Budgets, 5th Updated Edition | Deke Simon | $26.95
Film Production Management 101 | Deborah S. Patz | $39.95

DIRECTING | VISUALIZATION

Animation Unleashed | Ellen Besen | $26.95

Cinematography for Directors | Jacqueline Frost | $29.95
Citizen Kane Crash Course in Cinematography | David Worth | $19.95
Directing Actors | Judith Weston | $26.95
Directing Feature Films | Mark Travis | $26.95
Fast, Cheap & Under Control | John Gaspard | $26.95
Film Directing: Cinematic Motion, 2nd Edition | Steven D. Katz | $27.95
Film Directing: Shot by Shot | Steven D. Katz | $27.95
Film Director's Intuition, The | Judith Weston | $26.95
First Time Director | Gil Bettman | $27.95
From Word to Image, 2nd Edition | Marcie Begleiter | $26.95
I'll Be in My Trailer! | John Badham & Craig Modderno | $26.95
Master Shots | Christopher Kenworthy | $24.95
Setting Up Your Scenes | Richard D. Pepperman | $24.95
Setting Up Your Shots, 2nd Edition | Jeremy Vineyard | $22.95
Working Director, The | Charles Wilkinson | $22.95

DIGITAL | DOCUMENTARY | SPECIAL

Digital Filmmaking 101, 2nd Edition | Dale Newton & John Gaspard | $26.95
Digital Moviemaking 3.0 | Scott Billups | $24.95
Digital Video Secrets | Tony Levelle | $26.95
Greenscreen Made Easy | Jeremy Hanke & Michele Yamazaki | $19.95
Producing with Passion | Dorothy Fadiman & Tony Levelle | $22.95
Special Effects | Michael Slone | $31.95

EDITING

Cut by Cut | Gael Chandler | $35.95
Cut to the Chase | Bobbie O'Steen | $24.95
Eye is Quicker, The | Richard D. Pepperman | $27.95
Film Editing | Gael Chandler | $34.95
Invisible Cut, The | Bobbie O'Steen | $28.95

SOUND | DVD | CAREER

Complete DVD Book, The | Chris Gore & Paul J. Salamoff | $26.95
Costume Design 101, 2nd Edition | Richard La Motte | $24.95
Hitting Your Mark, 2nd Edition | Steve Carlson | $22.95
Sound Design | David Sonnenschein | $19.95
Sound Effects Bible, The | Ric Viers | $26.95
Storyboarding 101 | James Fraioli | $19.95
There's No Business Like Soul Business | Derek Rydall | $22.95
You Can Act! | D. W. Brown | $24.95

FINANCE | MARKETING | FUNDING

Art of Film Funding, The | Carole Lee Dean | $26.95
Bankroll | Tom Malloy | $26.95
Complete Independent Movie Marketing Handbook, The | Mark Steven Bosko | $39.95
Getting the Money | Jeremy Jusso | $26.95
Independent Film and Videomakers Guide – 2nd Edition, The | Michael Wiese | $29.95
Independent Film Distribution | Phil Hall | $26.95
Shaking the Money Tree, 3rd Edition | Morrie Warshawski | $26.95

MEDITATION | ART

Mandalas of Bali | Dewa Nyoman Batuan | $39.95

OUR FILMS

Dolphin Adventures: DVD | Michael Wiese and Hardy Jones | $24.95
Hardware Wars: DVD | Written and Directed by Ernie Fosselius | $14.95
On the Edge of a Dream | Michael Wiese | $16.95
Sacred Sites of the Dalai Lamas– DVD, The | Documentary by Michael Wiese | $24.95

To Order go to *www.mwp.com* or Call 1-800-833-5738